RUNNING

HOME AND AWAY

RUNNING
HOME AND AWAY

A COLLECTION OF RUNNING ADVENTURES

To my fellow scribe

Maggie

with best wishes

David Syme

COMPILED BY DAVID SYME

First published in 2012

ISBN 978-0-9543683-4-0

With thanks to The Partnership Publishing Solutions Ltd (project management)

Cover design by Caleb Rutherford – eidetic

Printed in the UK by Martins the Printers, Berwick upon Tweed

Contents

AWAY

This book is dedicated to the children of Tong-Len, Dharamsala, India.

May our efforts in writing it contribute to a better future for them.

Acknowledgements

I am very grateful to those who have encouraged and assisted me in the production of this book. My sister Helen Rainbow edited scripts scrupulously and offered sound advice, while Harmeny runner Alan Grierson of Bright Red Publishing convened an expert team to bring the project to reality. Caleb Rutherford's evocative cover designs will prompt many a purchase, while The Partnership's clear lay-out will ensure that reading this book will be a pleasant experience. A huge thank-you to all 13 fellow-contributors! The variety of running experiences and writing styles adds depth to the book. Some of their stories are humorous and exciting, some thought-provoking and instructional – all are inspirational! Finally I'd like to thank my wife, Pat. Having become accustomed to my absences on runs, she has also had to put up with many hours when I've been chained to the computer. I am deeply grateful for her tolerance and enthusiastic support.

Introduction

I am a keen runner who always seeks out an interesting route when away from home. As I do not use a camera I started writing up runs which seemed worth recording for later recall. This led to *Running Away From Home*, a collection of stories by myself, family and friends about runs in exotic locations which I published in December 2010. It prompted some readers to recall runs of their own which were worth describing, so I invited them to write to me with the story. Some did, and recommended others to do the same. As some wanted to describe runs in their country of residence (all UK except those of my son, Andrew, in Germany) I passed the word round that home-based stories would also fit into the sequel, hence the title of this collection, *Running: Home and Away*. I am fortunate to include stories from writers who have outstanding running pedigrees as well as runners who, like me, just like to 'go for a run'. The result is a diverse mix of locations, achievements and writing styles which, we hope, offers entertainment and inspiration to all runners.

As with *Running Away From Home* all royalties from the sale of this book will go to Tong-Len UK*, a charity which supports destitute children in Northern India, so please don't pass the book on – encourage others to buy their own copy!

*Tong-Len activities are described on page 173.

Foreword

Jonathan Wyatt

Photograph by Matthias Robl Photography, Schliersee, Germany

Jonathan, from New Zealand, has dominated world mountain running for the last 14 years.

I have travelled a lot. But not to places that most others will have gone to. It is running that has given me a reason to visit places I had never heard of before, and a chance to meet and stay with local people. It's given me plenty of stories and surprises along the way as well as a lot of friends in many different places; it's even given me my wife!

Running is the simple act of putting one foot in front of the other, with both feet off the ground at each stride. Racing is your ability to run a set distance at your optimum speed, giving you a time at the end of it. Taking part in races becomes a source of a lot of inspiration, fun and adventure.

I hope that this collection of stories will give you inspiration, fun and a desire to find your own running adventures.

HOME

24 hours in a Glasgow bar

Mark Cooper

Since Mark stopped smoking in 2007 he has tackled a string of huge physical challenges; the story below is an example. His achievements, his motivational speaker role and his contributions to worthy charities can all be seen at **www.runwithmark.com**

In truth I had unknowingly been training for this event for three years. I had run from Amsterdam to Barcelona, the width of the UK, cycled Land's End to John O' Groats and completed several ultra-marathon distances to be ready for this. On July 28th 2011 I stood in the bar of the Corinthian Club on Glasgow's Ingram Street. I was about to run on a treadmill for twenty four hours to raise money for a charity.

I have mixed emotions about the event, as usual with ultra runs I found it to be… very hard, not that hard, mentally taxing, amazing, frustrating and inspiring – all at the same time. Unless you have run ultras before it is hard to explain what goes through your head.

I arrived at the Corinthian Club on Wednesday morning for a photo call with Miss Scotland, we had a laugh with the treadmill and some jelly (Wobbly Williams being the charity) but at the back of my mind I knew what was about to happen, I knew the range of emotions I was about to go through and I could feel the familiar knot in my stomach which could only mean one thing; I was ready.

I always get this tight feeling in my gut before a big event, it means that I am fired up, prepared for the challenge. Earlier in the year I had attempted to run the West Highland Way Race. I suffered a Did Not Finish and it really rocked my confidence, it had never happened to me before. I was given a major boost when I completed the Trip to Remember at the start of July, a multi discipline event in which we cycled 50 miles, rowed the Irish Sea and walked 20 miles to the top of Snowdon within 35 hours. It was however my ability as an ultra-runner which had taken the knock and I was determined to finish this 24-hour event and prove to myself that I wasn't the kind of person who quits.

What followed for the next 24 hours was something that will stay with me for a long time.

Back in March I had completed a race called the d33, a relatively short ultramarathon event in Aberdeen. I had placed a respectable 23rd but had run out too fast. I ran the first 17 miles in under 2 hours and it took me 2 hours 30 minutes to finish the last 16 miles. After this experience I decided that I didn't want to do the 24hr treadmill event, purely because I didn't see the point of it, but the feeling of pain in my legs quickly passed and I carried on training as normal. Eventually I came to the realisation that I could do the treadmill run, as long as I didn't start off too quickly.

The treadmill had kindly been donated by the Edinburgh Marathon organiser, Neil Kilgour. I made sure that I took a few moments to myself before the event began, mainly to get my head in the right place but also to run through the game plan one last time. The longest I had ever run for – time wise – was seventeen hours, a year earlier to the day and I didn't know if I could manage it a year on. Extreme endurance events come down to stubbornness and that's the one thing I can normally pull out when it's needed. I would have no choice.

The horn rang out and I began running, the treadmill was set to 10 kilometres per hour and I started to stride out. Various people were there to see me start. Don Lennox who was planning to run across America in 2011 was there, so was Ian Goudie who had supported me in France during last year's Amsterdam to Barcelona run. The opening hour wasn't easy; I was struggling, there was no explanation for it, this was an easy pace for me. I got to two hours and I had to stop for a bathroom break. I rushed to the toilet and wished I had taken my Imodium. I was concerned to be experiencing bowel problems so early in the run; I had only done a half marathon! In my head at hour three I felt like I was getting nowhere, I punched the treadmill in anger. I had slowed my pace to eight kilometres per hour, then seven, then six but still I was struggling to keep up. I reached twenty-six kilometres in just over three hours and I was exhausted. My support team had been chatting amongst themselves and I was wondering what the subject of this secretive discussion was. It was only once I got to what I thought was forty five kilometres that I took a break. Bryn came over to me to have a quiet word.

Bryn was the main reason I undertook the event. He had been diagnosed with Parkinson's at 37. We met at a Jog Scotland awards ceremony, where we both won the Inspiration award and I was instantly impressed by his desire and courage. I have huge respect for Bryn. He set up his own charity called Wobbly Williams and I was now a part of that organisation; I was determined to do this for the cause.

"Mark," he said quietly, "I think the treadmill is actually set to miles per hour..."

After weighing up the fact that I was exhausted after what I thought was a just over a marathon distance and the fact that countless people had told me that I appeared to be running a little too fast, this would make sense. I couldn't believe it! I had run the opening twenty miles in two hours. I had never run twenty miles in two hours. What did I say about starting out too fast in a race? In any event it's madness in a twenty four hour one....

Thankfully, instead of finishing me off, this discovery had a positive impact on my mood. I had been on the floor thinking that I was making no progress and now I felt energised and alive. After seven hours I had run sixty miles, I was flying. There is always a merry-go-round of emotions running ultras and I had gone from the pits of hell to the highest heights and it felt good. The buzz of discovering I had run a load of miles instead of kilometres lasted for hours, I fed off it like a starving animal. I covered just shy of eighty miles in twelve hours and was on track for the world record (160.24 miles).

At hour twelve I decided to take five minutes to have a cheese sandwich and some crisps, all I had eaten so far was gels, cakes and energy drinks. I needed something that resembled real food. I chatted with my girlfriend Ferelith and good friend Lynne about my mental state and about how the adrenaline was now fading and was being replaced by doubt and pain. I slipped into a hole which lasted for three hours. There is nothing that anyone can say when this happens during an ultra, you have to get yourself out of it and the only way to do that is to keep on running. I had printed off some motivational quotes and pinned them to the front of the treadmill, one read, "You have a choice, you can throw in the towel or you can use it to wipe the sweat from your face," and another simply said, "Man up!" How true I thought.

I walked for thirty minutes. I didn't mind as I was still walking at a brisk four and a half miles per hour and feeling relatively fresh. It was now morning and the sun had risen on Glasgow, it felt good to have made it through the night. Bryn bought the morning papers and read out the various articles to me. Another boost was my friend Rhona coming through from Edinburgh to support me during the day. Lynne, who had been there all night, had gone to the hotel next door for some sleep and Ferelith had gone to work and would return with my Dad in the evening.

I didn't feel tired in the morning, probably due to all of the coffee I had been drinking. I ordered another double espresso from the bar and downed it. I hadn't eaten much but as usual I didn't feel like it.

I had decided to watch a few episodes of the American TV series *24* during the night and also some episodes of *Curb Your Enthusiasm*. For added inspiration I turned on the amazing film *Running the Sahara*, starring my buddy and all-round ultra-legend, Ray Zahab. Ferelith would later say that she had never seen me so happy, running while watching other people run. What can I say? I love to run!

Once it got to noon I really began to feel it. I had walked for a couple of hours now and even that began to hurt. My shoes were worn down at the back from the treadmill gradually sanding them down so I changed to another pair. The change felt good, they were very light and dry and gave my feet a new lease of life. The only problem with changing my shoes was that for the first time I felt the blisters. I hadn't felt any hot spots when running, but when I stopped to change they became painful. This might sound strange but the pain in my feet was a welcome distraction from the pain that had been building in my right knee for several hours. With three hours left on the clock Pamela Andrews came to see me. Pamela is a massage therapist and physio and I was grateful for her offer to help me out and more importantly her professional opinion. I lay down on the floor and she began massaging. You can imagine how tender my legs were for having run 105 miles. Ten minutes later, with a load of Tiger Balm on, I was back on the treadmill and heading for home, I had just over two hours left.

The room had been more or less empty on Friday. Rhona had been there and a few other people had popped their heads in to say hello, but it was actually nice to get my head down and not have to speak to anyone. I tend to go inside my own head when it gets hard and this suits me fine. With an hour to go I was flying. I had put the treadmill back up to seven miles per hour and had decided that I would run the last hour no matter what. Slowly the room began to fill. Sky Sports arrived, and a number of other photographers and journalists. I ignored them all, stared straight ahead and got on with business. Bryn told me with thirty minutes to go that I had run over two hundred kilometres! I was delighted, that was over 124 miles in twenty three and a half hours. I pushed on as fast as I could manage. With ten minutes to go the room was now packed and the atmosphere was amazing. What usually happens when I finish an event of my own making is that there are only one of two people there to clap me in. I don't do this for the applause but it felt good to have such great support. I upped the speed of the treadmill to ten miles per hour, exactly the speed I had started twenty four hours ago, coasting along with over one hundred and twenty eight miles in my legs. The crowd counted down to the final two minutes and at last 10, 9, 8, 7, 6, 5, 4, 3, 2, 1… 0!!! I punched the air, celebrating that I had managed it and also celebrating that it was finally over. Right away the Sky Sports cameras were in my face, various questions were asked, the main one being…

Q: Are you disappointed not to get the world record?
A: A world record is just a label, I don't need that to tell me I've done something pretty special here today.

I was presented with a glass of Guinness. I had been dreaming of this pint for the entire run. The pint disappeared very quickly and I stepped off of the treadmill. The final distance was 129.2 miles or 207.9 kilometres, just shy of five marathons. I left the room for a few minutes on my own and went to the bathroom. All through this event I had been going to the downstairs one, but now as I walked out of the crowded bar the concierge directed me to a bathroom on the same level as where I had been running – unbelievable! I collapsed on the floor and threw up the Guinness, I lay there shaking, unable to move for ten minutes, but I didn't care; I had managed what I set out to do... I hadn't known if I could, but I did it! I gathered myself, walked back into the room where all my friends were and joined them in celebrating another successful event. One hundred and twenty nine miles in twenty four hours meant that I had made it into the top ten of all time for this event (and I even beat celebrity runner Dean Karnazes' distance for his first attempt, not bad for an ex-smoker who used to run around the park with a smoke in his hand.)

"Unless you try to do something beyond what you have already mastered you will never grow."

That's damn right!

The 10k Taper

David Syme

The race was on Sunday morning; it was now the Thursday morning before. I had to go to my local village, East Calder, so I changed into my running kit. Fifteen minutes to the post office and chemists to pick up a prescription, then 15 minutes back, some pace variation using the distances between telephone posts perhaps, nothing strenuous, just an easing of the muscles in the wind-down before the race. Taper run, they call it.

It was cool and pleasant; a gentle breeze all that was left of the previous days' storms. The run to the shops was a slow but steady trot. The brain asked all parts of my body for injury reports, but none came. Wonderful! Anticipation of a race is a joy when you're feeling good, and I was feeling good. Letters posted, I entered the chemists to join a considerable queue of people at the counter, with more folk waiting for their prescriptions. I asked: "How long will my mine be?" The assistant waved a hand of explanation and apology briefly in the direction of the small crowd: "At least 40 minutes…" came the reply. A fractious child and a coughing adult helped me decide not to wait; I took a chit and left the shop.

I planned a pleasant, slow 40 minute run. On to Mid Calder, over the Almond and up to Pumpherston then right past the golf course and back along the old railway line. The roads were quiet and I enjoyed the smooth hard surface of the pavements until I turned down onto the path on the railway line. After only a few metres I had to go under the road bridge. But look! A huge puddle spread from one stone support across to the other. I approached cautiously and noticed that the wall on the left had a low shelf just below the water line. I edged my way along to the far end of the bridge and was wondering how to cross over the rest of the puddle to dry land when I heard a noise behind me. A runner came at full tilt; a slim, young sandy-haired lad – head up and arms pumping: Splash! Splash! Splash! Splash! And away! Wow! I stood open-mouthed, then a wave of embarrassment swept over me. What would he have thought of me? An old duffer dressed for a run, but scared of a wee dub! I started to run after him. I did not want to chase him and perhaps alarm him, so I held station with him, about 70 metres behind. I was now splashing through the puddles, too. The trouble was that this chap was much better than I, and my bid to demonstrate that I, too, could handle a bit of discomfort on a run was hurting. We sped down the railway path. I was pleased that he turned and saw me, hopefully recognising that I could run after all. He did not cross the viaduct, but dropped down to the river and turned downstream. I felt that I had not fully made my point, so followed him into Almondell Park. When he reached the main park road I was hoping that he would turn left, and that I could turn right and relax, but he turned right and started to lope up the long hill. I had to follow. This would show him that I wasn't to be underestimated! He must have known that I was using him as a pacer of sorts, and decided to see what I could do. Dog walkers looked at me with a mixture of curiosity, pity and amazement as I lumbered uphill at a pace which I would normally describe as my sprinting speed. When he reached the main road I could not have been more that 80 metres behind him, well maybe 100. He turned left, thank goodness, away from the chemist's, so when I reached the road I stopped and stood there panting. The lad turned and saw me, then waved and ran on. I managed a weak wave to his back then tottered on to the shop.

The crowd inside the shop was as before. When I entered, the sudden blast of hot air into my lungs brought on a coughing attack which, with my red face and mud-splattered clothing, ensured that I had as wide a circle of space round me as possible. I collected my prescription and, still coughing, limped home.

My performance on Sunday was poorer than I had hoped, but Thursday's run was one to remember because of the unexpected. I had been jolted out of a comfortable bimble by a runner who didn't worry about puddles. He caught me 'with my pants down' which showed me that I was getting soft. I had to prove to him and to myself that I could still run a bit, and really didn't mind the mud and the wet. The thrill of the chase and the satisfaction of keeping up with the young lad were worth it, but as a taper for the 10 km race it was a disaster!

Journey to Work:

The Rinderscharte Option

Andrew Syme

I live in Garmisch at 750 metres in the Bavarian Alps and work in Restaurant Alpspitz, which looks over the town at 2050 metres above sea level. My usual journey to work is by cable-car, but sometimes…

I rose at 6.15 am, took a light breakfast, then cycled to the cable car station, where I handed in my rucksack. It would be whisked up to the restaurant in twelve minutes. I tightened my trail shoes, took a deep breath, then started running.

The first part is flat; about 1.5km on a tarmac path along the valley floor which I always take gently as my warm-up, until I reach the sleepy village of Hammersbach.

This morning conditions were ideal for a run; heavy overnight rain had stopped but it was still overcast and, at about 15 degrees, considerably cooler than the last few days. Snatches of sun through the clouds gave hope for a fine day.

From Hammersbach the wide gravel path follows the river upstream with some steep sections until it reaches the Höllental Gorge Entrance Hut.

I overtook about twenty walkers who were starting their day in the mountains. After a quick 'How is business?' chat with the women who work at the hut I entered the gorge.

The gorge section lasts for 1.2km. It is a narrow path scooped out of the steep, grey chalk wall of the gorge, with sections of low-roofed tunnels joined by ladders and slippery wooden walkways. The constant roar of the river a few metres below reminds me that, while I am concentrating on safe passage, I am gaining height with every step.

After the overnight rain the whole gorge section was wet, water falling down at bathroom shower intensity and running along the path – in places ankle deep. With no way to avoid the cascades of water I just had to run through them, giving off involuntary yodelling gasps (great echo in the tunnels!) as the cold water ran down my neck. Running through these tunnels, slightly stooped due to the low roof, I felt a bit like a rat scurrying through a drain pipe! Despite the water it was enjoyable, with some steep steps and dramatic views of the angry river thundering through the narrow chasm.

Beyond the gorge the path zigzags then follows the river upstream, with fantastic views of the Zugspitze, Germany's highest mountain, and its glacier.

The zigzags took me high above the roaring stream, until a narrow path on a welcome flat section brought me to the Höllentalanger Hut, at about 1300 metres above sea level. A few climbers who had slept in the hut were on the terrace, binoculars trained on the route up to the Zugspitze.

At this point my path doubles back and I can see the flat section far below me.

I was now on a gently-sloping traverse on the south side of the mountain. With a steep drop down to the left I had to be careful about my footing – not only to avoid a fall but also due to the numerous alpine salamanders who seemed to find this path particularly inviting. These 10 centimetre long shiny black creatures were obviously in their mating season and had no problem with making a public affair of the occasion!

The path divides; both options would take me to the restaurant. The left leads onto a gradually-ascending path via the Knappenhäuser Hut, the right onto the steep, rocky path – the Rinderscharte.

This morning it had to be the Rinderscharte for me! Up I went on the steep zig-zag path over rock and loose stones, rapidly gaining height. Deep in thought and concentrating on my breathing and footing I was startled when three 'Gams' or wild mountain goats bolted off from close proximity with a strange hissing warning noise, leaving a strong goaty smell in the air.

The path became steeper and demanded more of a leap than a step but the biggest challenge was still to come. When my energy reserves were all but gone I reached the dreaded steps.

The path becomes so steep that steps have been built. Logs 50cm long have been pegged into the ground and loose gravel forms a natural platform.

Lots of them! I stopped counting after 132…. With a burning pain in my thigh muscles and cramp threatening my calf muscles, the end of the steps came not a moment too soon. I reached the top on a ridge then had to go down a short section on the other side. My legs didn't behave as I wanted them to; the muscles were still burning and bitterly complaining so I had a strange couple of minutes on very wobbly legs like a newly born calf taking its first steps!

The last bit of the run is a flat section towards the building with the cable car station and Restaurant Alpspitz.

I passed walkers who had taken the early cable car and were now setting off to climb the famous rocky pyramid of the Alpspitze. With feelings of relief and satisfaction verging on joy I reached the building – my finishing line – at 8 am; behind me 11.5 kilometres and 1400 metres climbed.

The restaurant serves fresh hot food all day, and there is a terrace with dramatic views over the mountains.

What now for me? Maybe a beer sitting in the sunshine, a well earned breakfast, a relaxing couple of hours in a sun lounger? Some chance! After a quick shower it was nine hours on my feet serving food and drink to hungry climbers and tourists. I had no choice; after all this had been my journey to work. Although I had a long, hard day I kept thinking how special my journey was, in comparison with many other commutes – by car, train or bus, and how lucky I was to have this option. The memories from my happy run, alone on the mountain, kept a smile on my face all day, but the next morning I took the cable car!

I Run, I Dream

David McKendrick

I am a dedicated but somewhat rubbish distance runner. PB for 10k is fifty minutes, but have gone up to half marathon and hold out some hope for twenty-six point two. Away from running I lecture at Glasgow Caledonian University and spend the rest of my time with my wife and family. Soul music fan.

If I am being completely honest I would have to admit to being a bit of a dreamer. Quite an admission from a forty-two year old father of four. You would think I have little enough time to dream what with work, home life and all of the other things that go on, but I am and I always have been a dreamer.

It might well come from a fertile imagination. All those years of reading books has made me quite an imaginative wee soul. Running has not helped either – in fact it has done quite the opposite – it has encouraged it, made me even more of a dreamer, even more imaginative.

I am a determined but rubbish distance runner. I run for a number of reasons, but one of the primary ones is that my other interests centre around sitting down. I like to sit in a number of places. My local Indian restaurant for one… or Kelly's Bar in Cleland… or my favourite of all, the chair in the living room. Ask my wife she'll tell you: I can sit anywhere. So running is an antidote to sitting but it provides me with something else, something most runners seem to thrive on, the opportunity to test myself, to see how far or fast I can run. In my case distance is the thing. I can run a half marathon alright, but I dream one day of a marathon. I dream more specifically of the Rome Marathon.

Some runs make this dream seems like more of a distant hope.

As I lumber about the streets of Wishaw and Newmains at an appallingly slow pace I wonder if I'll ever do it. No I don't wonder, I am fairly confident that it is beyond me. Sometimes I catch sight of myself in a shop window. I seem to run from the knees down, my upper body is rigid, my arms bent at the elbows, moving imperceptibly to boost my minimal speed. A marathon? You must be daft, if I can get home without collapsing I'll be happy.

But inspiration is never far away. I think of my good friend Eric. An ex Para, a racing snake, all legs and elegant technique. You name the race – he's run it, Marathon Des Sables? Yip. De'il o' the Highlands, completed. You name it, he's done it. Usually in some sexy time, never injured, always up for it… makes you sick.

Or that Andrew Murray, Scotland to Sahara. More ultra marathons than you can shake a stick at. I followed him on Twitter (still do in fact), the kids and I would send him messages, he became a celebrity in our house. We were so chuffed when he finished, we had a wee party for him; it was a major event in our house. Whenever he is on the telly we gather round, there is a hushed silence, even Henrik Larsson doesn't get that.

Both of these guys are an inspiration to me. Although I am a dreamer I am honest enough to know that my age and lifestyle make in unlikely I'll ever run 26.2 miles. To do that I would need to change my lifestyle, find the time to increase my training, sit a bit less (especially in pubs and Indian restaurants) and this change is just too big for me. I am happy with my running. Well, as happy as any runner can be.

But this is where that strange but joyful running synergy occurs. Sometimes when I am out running I dream I am Andrew Murray or Eric. As I puff up a hill into Shotts I imagine I am Andy Murray running through the snow in France. As I pass the dilapidated ruin of Hartwood hospital on a damp, dark Monday morning I imagine I am in the baking heat of the Sahara, testing myself against the finest endurance athletes there are. Of course, I know I am not. I am rubbish but determined. I am not in the Sahara, I'm in Lanarkshire. I know this.

But I can and do dream. There are similarities. I am a runner just like the greats. Others, non runners are in their beds, on crowded buses, in cars with the red light on the petrol gauge. Me? I am out there just like Eric or Andy, with my Asics on my feet, my Under Armour and my running shorts. I have learned from them. I have the Vaseline on, and I have taken plenty of water. If I feel good I know I can attempt a fartlek (attempt, not complete) I can taper. I know the jargon. I am a runner. I have even had runner's high! In the end, in my head, there are more similarities than differences. I know this.

Just because you are not the best runner does not mean you are the worst. Personally I think I might well be one of the worst, but for a brief moment, while the rest of my life waits for me to get back to it, I am up there running through the Sahara, through the high Atlas Mountains, taking on all kinds of terrain, crossing the finish line in Rome. Only, if you see me I am the tubby, red-faced bloke waddling around Shotts and Newmains or struggling up the hill from Wishaw to Cambusnethan. But hey, I am a runner, I can dream.

Can't you?

Tow Path Dwam

David Syme

Dwam or dwaum (Scots): a stupor or a daydream as in 'to be in a dwam'.

I ran along a quiet section of the Union Canal near Ratho the other day. There is little charm about the towpath at the end of the year. On one side – the still, greeny-brown canal behind dry reeds, on the other – bare trees or a brambly hedge with dull winter farmland beyond. With few people about it is a perfect setting for a runner to enjoy a good dwam.

As I relaxed into the run, the dwam invaded my mind like a sea mist. I started thinking about Dundee High School Former Pupils' Rugby Club. This is not as weird as it may seem, as I had watched their team play at Currie the day before, and was impressed by their standard of play. I remember their teams in the 60s, when we used to come south from Aberdeen for a game. Then, they were about our level, which was not very high. But, of course later on they had had some useful players! Who could forget David Leslie, a great back-row forward in the 70s or Andy… what is his surname? He played scrum half, and we all remember the picture of him holding up the Calcutta Cup with a bleeding nose. That would be about ten years ago. What was his name now…? Good lad, if I remember, and plucky. Works as a TV pundit and commentator now. What's his name again?

In a dwam you are never in a hurry, so I plodded along the path, occasionally deflected from my reverie by a passing cyclist

or dog-walker, and tried to tease out that surname. Andy A...,
Andy B..., Andy C... No, I went all the way through the alphabet
without the flashing light of success. My next tactic was to pretend
to be thinking about something else, then return to the forename
quickly, blurting out what came into my head. Andy Pandy! No...
Andy Murray! No... Andy Irvine! No, but getting closer. Andy
Irvine! Now there was a rugby player; you never knew what you
would get when he was in the national team, but he was one of the
first full-backs to offer a threat in attack... Andy Williams! No, off
the scent again.

I knew that I was approaching a route decision point, so
turned my attention to the run. Should I plod on, or should I
break the monotony of the towpath for a mile or so by taking an
'add-on'? The hypnotic power of the dwam won easily, so I stuck
to the towpath and returned to the task of remembering Andy's
surname. Andy...? A cyclist approached, and I had half a mind to
stop him and ask if, by any chance, he knew the name of a recent
Scottish scrum half, first name Andy, but as he drew nearer I
recognised the no-nonsense, get-out-of-my-way body language of
some cyclists and held my tongue. He sped past.

Should I buy a bike? This is a recurring theme, and good
dwam material. Cycling! Doesn't it look great on a fine, windless
day! As a break from running, why not try a cycle trip? With a
bike you can go much further, see more, it's good exercise, and
handy for popping down to the local shops. My mind drifted to
bikes I had owned in the past, what had become of them, what
trips I had enjoyed, and then, to stop myself getting carried away,
I looked at the downside. Battling into gale-force winds, my talent
for finding sharp objects which puncture tyres... Do I really want
to go through all that again? There's plenty to do besides cycling...
Unless I concentrated on down-wind cycling on a bike with thick
tyres! With an eye on the weather charts and a rail card it should

be possible to find a route which is down-wind all the way. We could have a Downhill Only Cycling Club – DOCC has a nice ring to it. What did I do with my last bike, the hybrid? I gave it to Peter Robertson's son, who had come to Edinburgh as a student. What was he called again? Nicol, that was it, Nicol Robertson… Just a minute! Andy Nicol! The surname of the rugby player had crept up in the guise of a Christian name.

That was the curtain call at the end of the dwam; a successful recall and not 5 minutes before I reached home. I switched the brain back into reality, and cruised home with a smile on my face.

Andy Nicol… of course… Andy Nicol.

West Highland Way Race

18th June 2011

Donald Sandeman, Harmeny Athletic

---

55 years old and served as a police officer for 30 years, now a part-time cabbie in Edinburgh. Always been very keen on travel to the less touristy parts of the world. Took up running aged 43 having retired with injuries from rugby. Started with marathons but got fed up with tarmac so moved on to ultras. Always looking for new challenges...
Hardest races so far in order: MDS in 2006, West Highland Way 2011 and CCC (Ultra Tour de Mont Blanc) in 2007.
Presently do around four marathons and eight ultras per year.
Marathon PB 3.11 but getting a lot slower.

What is the Next Great Challenge once you have a few 'ordinary' marathons, then the Marathon des Sables behind you? After a few quiet years I set my sights in 2011 on completing Scotland's West Highland Way Race in 24 hours. With 95 miles to run and 14,760 ft of ascent it qualifies as a Great Challenge in my book, and it's in my own back garden. It's a long race, so this is a long story.

My training was going well until November, when something in my calf twanged and took ages to fade away. A sports masseur cured it eight days before our club's excursion to the Marrakesh Marathon in January, and, after a very quick train and taper I got round the course uninjured and in a reasonable time. There followed some training runs in the Pentlands, some runs over part of the West Highland Way course and some ultras. Some friends thought I was overdoing the ultras, but good times and no injuries gave me confidence that I could beat 24 hours for the race.

The rules state that you have to have a motorised back-up

team with a runner capable of searching for you if you go missing. You may have a support runner from half-way if you are more than 4 hours behind the leader. The support team makes a huge commitment, giving up their weekend and two nights of sleep. I was fortunate that wife Elaine and good friends Derek and Shona volunteered; doubly fortunate that Derek and Shona own a motor-home the size of Eddie Stobart's biggest truck! So the team was exclusively runners from Harmeny, my running club. We stripped the Tesco shelves of junk food, and I made up a monster tub of my secret weapon: a slurry of cold, salty, cheesy mashed potato with baked beans. A favourite of mine but most people – even pigs – would pass on it!

The race starts at 01.00 am at Milngavie railway station. As we were only faffing about we went early, with plenty of time for registration and weigh-in. (The weighing is repeated at several points in the race to make sure weight does not vary too much.) We retired to the motor-home for caffeine and Vaseline-rubbing, then mingled with other teams. The ultra-running community is a small but friendly one; you end up knowing just about everyone else. The safety briefing was at 12.30 am, adjustment of pack and head-torch, and I found myself retching and shaking. I immediately felt better when the hooter sounded, and I set off with another 153 adrenalin-fuelled runners. Game on!

The first section of 12.5 miles to Drymen is easy running; a line of head-torches snaking through the gloom. Passing Dumgoyne I stumbled on a downhill stretch and did a somersault, luckily landing on soft grass, uninjured. As I swopped trees for open moorland on the climb of Conic Hill I could switch off the head-torch, although the summit was shrouded in low cloud. On the descent the clouds parted to reveal Loch Lomond with its islands. I stopped for a wee moment to drink in the view, then continued down at a steady pace, saving my quads for later.

The first section ended with a pit-stop at Balmaha; I was bang on time at 04.35 am. The next leg to Rowardennen was excellent, with great scenery, total stillness, and I never saw another runner! My stomach was beginning to play up, but I put that down to running a very hilly marathon and eating food at silly o'clock. Elaine helped me eat and change socks, then I faced 25 miles without the support team. Stomach cramps hit me hard, and I had three trips to the bracken, giving the midges a breakfast feast of my bum. I walked for a while, and calm returned to my stomach, so was feeling much better when I reached Inversnaid. The Trossachs Search and Rescue Team were manning a food station of drop bags here. With midge nets over their heads they looked like Grim Reapers. I could see the reason for the nets. When I stopped to eat my slurry a swarm of midges descended on it, so I decided to eat on the move. This section is rocky and hilly, but I felt fine and reached the next checkpoint at Auchtertyre only 10 minutes behind schedule, so quite pleased. Also pleased when the scales showed my weight to be spot-on. The next 3 miles were an easy lope over to Tyndrum, where the team were waiting with more food.

After Tyndrum the rain became heavier, and the headwind stronger. Halfway to Bridge of Orchy my right foot and ankle began to get really sore, and I struggled on the downhill stretches. When I limped in to the station my team set about me like a Formula 1 pit team, massaging Ibuprofen into my legs, feeding me painkillers and food and changing my clothes. I set off up the hill feeling much better, but, unfortunately, the downhill parts had me in pain again. I was hoping I could run through it, but it didn't happen. At Victoria Bridge (more food and First Aid) I realised that a sore foot and 35 miles still to run added up to missing my target time of 24 hours.

Even to write about the last sections brings a tear to my eye…

My running pace had deteriorated to a shuffling jog. I felt pain at every step and squirmed, puffed and groaned my way forward. At Kinlochleven the excellent fish supper did its best to raise my morale. I ate it in the motor-home, hiding from the race doctor in case he saw my condition and binned me. It was dusk as I left the checkpoint and tackled the steep climb to the Lairig Mhor. Three splashes of orange light marked points manned by the Wilderness Response Team. These guys were great, giving out drinks and chocolate and morale-raising encouragement. At the last point I asked how far still to go to to Lundavra, the last checkpoint, and was told 4 miles. Thank goodness the darkness hid my tears. When I reached Lundavra with its blazing bonfire I did not stop. I knew that if I did I would find it very, very difficult to go on, and there were still 7 miles between me and the Finish. As I neared the Finish Elaine ran alongside me. I could see a runner behind me, and said that I was determined not to let him pass me. Elaine argued that one place didn't matter, and for the good of my health I should slow down… avoid permanent damage… take it easy…

The 'difference of opinion' between us spurred me on, and I broke into a shambling run. Derek and Shona joined us and we all crossed the line after 27 hours 45 minutes and 30 seconds. There followed a few communal tears, a large dram from the quaich and a shower. When taking off my right shoe and sock I noticed that my foot resembled a red balloon. Derek had to help me shower, dress me then lug me to the motor-home, where I crashed out with an ice pack on the foot. I awoke at 09.00 to the spluttering of frying bacon and of Derek, excited about a girl changing her top in the car-park.

The prize-giving was an emotional event for all who had been involved. In bright sunshine, every finisher's name was announced and a crystal goblet was presented. The loudest cheers were kept for those who had been on the course longest. There followed a great party in the Ben Nevis bar, and, for me, a trip to the local hospital An X-ray revealed a hairline fracture of the tibula and associated damage to tendons. I was told that – should it happen again – best not to run a further 45 miles on it.

So, a tough race. Forty fit and determined athletes did not make it to the Finish. I did, thanks largely to my support crew. I needed them much more than anticipated, and they went out of their way to be super-efficient. It was a privilege to take part in a race with some of the finest people I have ever met, and, as an achievement, it is right up there with the Marathon des Sables. Would I do it again? You bet I would!

Hamburg Marathon:

When it all goes well (22nd April 2001)

Andrew Syme

Andrew took the club bus from Garmisch to Hamburg for the marathon.

A double seat! Thank goodness – had a bit of a scare when more people got on in Munich but through good luck (or the way I look!) nobody wanted the seat next to me. We had started the journey on time at 8 pm leaving Garmisch in falling snow and the temperature hovering around the freezing mark. Sitting in the seat in front of me was my friend Danny. We chatted for a couple of hours, mostly about running and nutrition. He runs a fruit and veg shop and argues that the only way to live healthily is to eat only fruit and veg, with the occasional (two or three times per year) two week fasting period. After 4 hours' driving we had a one-hour toilet stop; a chance to stretch the legs and to mingle with some of the others on the bus. The last bit of the journey was a case of making yourself as comfortable as possible and trying to get some sleep.

I dozed on and off, then was awake to watch a stunning sunrise at about 6 am. We pulled up to the holiday Inn, Hamburg at 7.30 am, and were delighted to be given our room keys straight away. I was in a room with Danny, but to our horror we found ourselves with a fairly small double bed. I explained to Danny that I liked him but that I had to draw a line somewhere. He agreed, so after a worrying 10 minute wait at reception (Hamburg was full!) we were given a room with two beds. Breakfast was the usual nice buffet then most of us walked along Keiler Street to the nearest S-bahn station and went to the Trade Fair halls to collect start numbers etc. There was a lot going on at the halls with a kiddies' run, an inline skater race as well as all the promotions and stalls. I collected my start number and time chip which is always quite an emotional event for me considering my first marathon attempt, when I missed registration and could not take part. At this point the group dispersed as people followed their instincts for the rest of the day. The majority went on a bus sight-seeing tour which I had done so I just wandered around the stalls then went to St Pauli's football stadium. They were playing that afternoon but the game was sold out. I headed back to the hotel, stopping for lunch on the way. I had a nice nap in the afternoon then had an early supper in the hotel, it was ideal, a pasta buffet. I ate as much as I could then went back to the room in time to watch the football round-up on TV. I went to bed at about 9.30 pm but it took me ages to get to sleep due to nerves and the busy traffic on the main road.

The wake up call at 6 am. I was in a nice dream then, so it was quite a shock to realise I had 42 kilometres to run today! I put my running kit on, packed then went down to breakfast. I managed to force down a couple of rolls then checked out and got on the bus at 7.30 am. The weather was ideal! While it was still snowing in Garmisch, in Hamburg we had clear skies, a light wind and a temperature of about 3C. The bus dropped off the 15 of us who were runners and we made our way to the halls. As usual I had to join one of the monster queues for the toilet then warmed up, stripped off and handed in my bag. We made our way to the start, Danny and I were in the A block and decided to start together. Standing at the start and feeling good is for me a great moment. I felt that the training had gone well, I'd rested well in the last week, I was happy and confident about my shoes, my stomach felt settled and comfortably full and now it was simply a case of running and enjoying it. As the seconds counted down the 7,000 runners in my block started a slow hand clap which speeded up and ended with a cheer as the start gun went off.

It took Danny and me about two minutes to cross the start then we were off. Through the red-light district of the Reeperbahn (past the women showing off their breasts) and then down to the fish market. We got into a steady rhythm, the first kilometre was in 5 minutes but then as the field spread out a bit we were able to pick up the pace. The organizers had come up with the good idea of starting the three blocks with 5 and 10 minute gaps to try to reduce congestion at the beginning and it worked superbly, despite the additional 4,000 runners compared to last year. We hit the 10km mark in 46.30 minutes which was a good 2.3 minutes faster than last year. I was feeling okay but a bit wary about the long distance still ahead. Danny kept powering on and certainly kept me going at a faster pace than if I had been running on my own. It's thanks to him that I got a respectable time! We did the second 10km in 44.3 minutes, Danny said he was feeling good and that he was within his optimal heart rate level, but I could see he was starting to tire; he was landing flat-footedly and he was panting quite heavily. I made a point of taking water at every occasion it was offered and also took bits of banana for energy. We got to the half way point in 1hr 35mins so I was confident of achieving my target time of 3hrs 10mins. At about 25km I lost Danny but was still feeling good. I kept the thought in my head that a marathon really starts at the 30 km mark. The crowd was sensational, at times we would come around a corner and see a long stretch with crowds four or five deep on both sides cheering as though St Pauli had just scored the winning goal in the Champions League final! Between the 31st and 33rd km I passed two runners from the bus who I thought would beat me. I think both had started too fast, one of them told me later that they did the 1st 10 km in 38mins and now they were stiff and cramping up. Although I still felt OK, between the 35th and 40th km I started to tire but maintained my km times of about 4 mins 10–20secs. I passed the 40 km mark in 2hrs 57.44 and realised I was on for a good time and that nothing could go wrong now.

Running along the finishing straight was the usual fantastic experience, and, not for the first time that day, I got goose bumps which started at the top of my head and sent shudders down my back! 3 hrs 6 mins. I didn't feel bad at the finish, in earlier marathons I often felt dizzy and sick at the end but to my relief I felt fine. I collected my bag, had a shower (cold!), then watched others finishing.

The bus left at 3.30 pm, 30 minutes later than planned, but that's almost become the norm as people can't find the bus! It was interesting to talk and hear about other people's experiences, some who were disappointed and trying to work out why they hadn't met their goals and others, especially the first timers, were over the moon at just finishing. Danny, who was only a couple of minutes behind me at the 30th km mark, struggled at the end due to cramp but still finished in a good time of 3hrs 26mins. The bus journey back was a bit of a slog, we had a break after 5 hours for some much-needed food then most people slept or dozed until arriving safely (thanks Bernd) in Garmisch at 2 am.

I certainly enjoyed the weekend and it was a huge relief to knock eleven minutes off my PB. I had used the large amounts of free time in March and April for marathon training so it was gratifying to see that it had paid off.

Who knows if I will ever be able to enter a marathon as well trained as for this one…

When all does not go to plan: My first Ironman

Frank Tooley

As well as being a strong and enthusiastic runner with Harmeny, Frank has branched into triathlons.

The jinx started in July when I crashed badly on the last cycle training before my first Iron Man event, Outlaw in Nottingham. I broke a collar bone and damaged my ankle, knee, hip and elbow from scraping across the road. Thanks to great physio and a lot of work I was ready only 10 weeks later for my next first attempt at the Iron Man: Challenge Henley.

It started at 6.30 am on Sunday, so I was dropped off by Susan, my wife, at Henley Business School at 5.30, temperature 5.5 degrees. I took the rain cover off my bike and filled bottles then met the first challenge of the day, a flat front tyre. No problem, as I had in the bike bag two tubes which had been checked for leaks. It was pitch dark so I borrowed a head torch, changed tube, pumped it up with a borrowed track pump and still had plenty of time to put on calf guards and wetsuit, drop off outer clothes and rush to the start… only to find it delayed by 10 minutes due to lack of visibility till 6.40! Everyone was shivering by the time we entered the Thames but at last the hooter sounded, we were off and the six months of waiting were behind me. The water temperature was okay at 15 degrees compared to the Scottish reservoir I had trained in, but the water tasted of petrol.

My right goggle soon filled with water but I breathe to the right on every second stroke (I have asthma and can't manage bilateral breathing) so this wasn't an issue for sighting. I swam on the left as my right arm is still weak and ended up swimming along the line of buoys marking the furthest left you were allowed to go. This was into the current on the way out and also out of the current on the way back – talk about making things difficult for yourself! I didn't push it at all as I was still a bit concerned about my arm and hadn't done longer than 2 km since the accident. Both calves cramped badly towards the end, but if you just keep swimming that passes in a few minutes and you can kick again. I was really worried when the marshal almost pulled my bad arm out its socket to 'help' me out the river after 1hr 13 mins.

I was very cold as I collected the bag, took a swig of flat coke to kill any bugs (subsequently I would learn that lots of people were off work Mon–Wed with Thames tummy), stripped in a tent then put on my cycling stuff – my transition time was 400th fastest. I put on merino socks, shoes and neoprene shoe covers to try to get some warmth back in feet. On collecting the bike I was relieved to see both tyres still inflated and switched on the computer – all readings were at zero! I did all my training with a heart rate monitor and intended to cycle at 140–150 bpm but no readings? I would just have to go by feel. The first lap of 38 miles with 600 metres of ascent was fine. A bit scary seeing the ambulance go past a couple of times but I was cycling well – 2 hours. I stopped at least once per lap to fill my water bottle and go for a pee and noticed in horror that others were peeing on the bike – something I'd read about as being done by proper racers but I'd never seen in a race before. I stopped at the special needs area to say, 'hi' to Susan and fill my Bento box with home-made flap-jacks, which I was diligently eating at 100 calories every 20 minutes, and started the second lap.

A spoke broke and my rear punctured. I didn't have a long valve tube and was using deep rim wheels so had to use a valve extender to pump it up. The tiny o-ring needed for this was still on the front tyre. When I got it off, I lost it, probably because my hands were still frozen. So I was stuck not being able to pump the tube up – a rookie mistake. I had to wait for a motorbike bike mechanic and he got his CO_2 pump over the small bit of the valve that poked through the rim so I was going again… for about 200 yards. The rear punctured again but by now I had no tubes left, no pump, no CO_2 left. A sane person would have accepted defeat at this point and probably thrown the bike in a hedge. No way after all that physio was I giving up, so I thought: lots of people will puncture – I'll pass someone soon and beg them for a tube and pump. However, everyone else was having better luck and I cycled for 15 miles with a flat rear (don't try it as it destroys your rim!) until I found Tony Rutter of Alnwick Tri at the side of the road who had a broken skewer so had retired. He gave me a long-valve tube and a CO_2 and when I changed tube for third time I noticed I had a broken spoke so Tony suggested I bend it out of the way. I was going again. However the wheel was shaped like a 50p coin and I was terrified the other 19 spokes were going to go and the wheel collapse so I took it really slowly on descents. My wife was very pleased to see me complete the second lap eventually and I got a spare tube and CO_2 so that if I had a fourth flat I could change it. I was sure for most of the ride that I was going to have to retire so I was really amazed to finish, albeit in a downpour that meant the road was like a river and I was cycling down hill with both brakes on at the same speed I could go up it! The cycling phase took 7 hours.

The second transition was another faff, complete strip to change into comfortable running kit. Then only the small matter of a marathon to run… I didn't feel like eating at this stage so I survived on a combination of gels, flat coke, bananas and High Five. Four laps of 10.5 km and conditions were ideal, no wind, cool enough to just wear my Harmeny vest and almost completely flat as we ran beside the Thames. I walked a bit of the last lap as I found a Stirling tri guy to chat to and stopped on each lap to say hi to Susan who told me as I was about to start last lap that I should stop and eat something as I looked really grey and ill – thanks! I finished at sunset just when they were switching on floodlights. I did my slowest ever marathon: 4.31.

I ran through the finishing arch to be presented with a medal by the winner of the women's race. A respectable 13.05 hours total including transitions. I proceeded to the massage area to have my calves worked on for 10 minutes, no food left in the athletes' rest area so after eventually finding my bike in the dark transition area, I had carry-out chicken burger and chips from a greasy spoon café on the drive back to our hotel.

Didn't really sink in what I'd done till a few days after when I realised that completing this was my proudest personal achievement since I left academia 11 years previously. However, I'm not happy with making such a mess of the ride so I just bought new tubes, new tyres, a puncture repair kit, a pump, five CO_2 cartridges and booked up to do Outlaw next year!

Blessed are the Pathmakers

David Syme

At the end of June I was mopping up unclimbed Munros in the Cairngorms, and set out to climb Ben Avon (pronounced Arn). This hill is a big one – at 1171 metres above sea level the 16th highest in Scotland and a long way from anywhere. I approached from Deeside. As I parked at Invercauld the strong wind prompted two thoughts: Firstly, great – no midges! Secondly, will I be able to stand up on the summit plateau?

I started on a tarmac road through the estate, passing well-kept gardens and acres of short grass in front of the 'Big Hoose'. The road became a track as I turned for the Sluigain, a long glen well-known to generations of climbers heading for the rock faces of Beinn a' Bhuird and Ben Avon. The glen ends above a ruined lodge, and as I climbed over the bealach (saddle) into upper Glen Quoich the north wind hit me hard. The short grass was rippling like water and the buffeting gusts were hitting me face-on. The frowning cliffs of Beinn a' Bhuird were only half-visible as low cloud swept over the upper ramparts. The only positive aspect was that the path had become excellent! It was almost flat; a ribbon of pink granite sand, broken every few metres by well-constructed drainage channels. I continued for a mile or so, hoping for signs that it would become calmer, but no, the wind force seemed to be set at howling gale. After 20 minutes of sheltering behind a boulder I turned back.

Ten days later I was back, encouraged by a positive weather forecast of light winds and clear skies. Again I parked at Invercauld, but this time I was dressed in my running gear; Salomon trail shoes and frameless day-sack, Ron Hill long-sleeved top, Skinfit thigh-length shorts and Chaskee cap. I also tied a large handkerchief round my neck. I carried no water, just my plastic mug, as I find the burn water of the Cairngorms excellent to drink. In high spirits I loped along the road, turned up the track and was soon eating up the long miles of the Sluigain. I couldn't wait to get on that pink ribbon! I reached it and settled into a comfortable stride. The hilltops were clear, and I enjoyed great views of Beinn a' Bhuird, at the same time taking care not to tumble into the drainage channels. As I had driven up from Edinburgh I was not the first on the hill, and as I reached the start of the steep section I caught up with an English couple who were heading (slowly) for a climb in Garbh Coire. We chatted then I trotted onwards and upwards. At the path junction (left for Beinn a' Bhuird, right for Ben Avon) I swung right and picked my way up zig-zags of loose scree until I reached the plateau. This is a tree-less expanse of stony ground with tussocks of hardy grasses and mosses and several knobbly tors of granite. The highest was less than 1 km away, and it was a delight to run almost level until the last 100 metres or so, where an easy rise led to the rocks. Once on top I relaxed to take in the view; the near hills of Lochnagar, Hill of Fare and Bennachie stood out but further away the clarity was lost in a shimmering haze. I nibbled some nuts and raisins, phoned home, then retraced my steps. It had taken me 3 hours to reach the summit, and I was confident of knocking some time off that on the descent. With a broad smile on my face I ran over the plateau, ran and slid down the zig-zags and, at the path junction, met the English couple. They told me that they had spent the night at the Sluigain howff, and at some unspecified time there had become engaged. The howff is a small wooden-floored shelter scarcely 1 metre high, tucked away in a quiet side glen – hardly the most likely venue for an engagement. Perhaps the implications of this dramatic event explained their slow progress uphill. I sped down the steep section and found an easy rhythm on the pink ribbon, which had some of the qualities of a cinder track. All too soon I was on the rocky track of the Sluigain once more, where the lack of any wind and the strong sun sapped my energy. I changed down a gear, running on the flat and downhill, but slowing to a fast walk on even the gentlest of uphill stretches. The estate road seemed longer than on the way up, but I reached my car just over 5 hours after leaving it.

I had been disappointed to have to turn back on my earlier attempt at this mountain, but the pleasure of running up and down it in benign conditions more than made up for it. I am nearly finished my round of the Munroes and my days on some hills are hard to recollect. Ben Avon stands out as special; that beautiful path through Glen Quoich gave me a purple passage of running in spectacular scenery. I won't forget that in a hurry!

Wet Feet – The Black Rock '5'

Ann Davidson

As a child, Ann was not what you would call 'sporty', in fact she was more 'the wee wheezy kid who's always last'. As an adult she eventually agreed to try jogging after years of insistence from friends and particularly her sister that she would enjoy it. Numerous 10ks, half marathons and nine marathons later, it looks like they might be right! Ann became the jogscotland Programmes Coordinator in 2007. jogscotland is Scotland's national recreational running network encouraging people of all abilities to get and stay active through jogging and running.

The Black Rock '5' race is an unusual event that takes place every year in the Fife village of Kinghorn. Well, actually most of it takes place on the beach beyond the village. The distance is described as 'approximately 5 miles' and the race always takes place on a Friday night but the date varies between May and July to reflect variations in the tides. The race entry form carries the warning, 'You will get your feet wet'. Undeterred, I decided to submit my entry.

The evening of the race was bright but a bit breezy and we all gathered below the railway bridge slightly reluctant to head up the hill to the start line. When the starter horn sounded we surged forward and the fastest runners quickly reached the top of the hill leaving us lesser mortals struggling uphill to the main road. It was a relief to reach the corner and start on our way to the beach. The route wound its way through the village, gradually leading downhill. Many of the local residents had turned out to support the event and offer encouragement along the way.

I arrived at the beach to see a line of runners heading out into the distance. It looked such a long way to the 'Rock' but there was no time to worry about that now. As soon as I hit the sand my legs felt much heavier and it got much harder to lift my feet as I jogged towards the water. However, very soon I was on the firm, damp sand that had been exposed by the receding tide and running became slightly easier. I hadn't anticipated the effect of the tide on the sand though. Far from being a smooth surface, the sand had formed into ripples which could all too easily cause a twisted ankle. I hadn't been going fast before but now I eased off, trying to disregard the front runners who were strung out in a long line well into the distance. I also found that the wind was getting much stronger as I made my way further away from the relative shelter of the beach.

At first I tried to dodge the puddles but then I realised that I really was going to get my feet wet and accepted I'd just have to splash my way through them. As I got further away from the beach there were fewer patches of sand and ever larger puddles until I was paddling along. As I got closer to the rock I began to hear bagpipe music. Sure enough, there was a piper in full formal attire standing on top of the rock and playing his pipes!

By the time I reached the rock we were all wading through knee deep water and I heard the group of ladies behind me talking about what a bizarre experience this was. At that point one of them took her mobile phone out of her pocket and got her friends to stop so she could take a photograph of them all standing knee deep in the Forth beside the Black Rock. I splashed on knowing I wouldn't be last – provided they didn't catch up with me.

As I turned back towards the beach it was great to find that the wind was now behind me but it looked a long way to the village. A few hardy souls had headed out on to the sand to encourage the runners. Their support was very welcome.

I was so glad to get back to the beach feeling that there wasn't far to go but I hadn't reckoned on how hard it was to run through dry sand wearing wet trainers. That was a slog, and the ramp from the beach up to the street, although short, was a sharp reminder that I really should have done more training for this event.

The course led back along the road through the village and it was good to be running on an even surface again, although the combination of sand-filled shoes and wet socks felt a bit uncomfortable. I was finally able to relax slightly as I headed downhill to the railway bridge where the race had started. The helpful marshals standing there advised, 'the finish is just round the corner'. Well, yes it is but it's at the top of a very steep hill! However, by this point there were lots of cheering spectators shouting encouragement so I just had to keep going, although I felt I was running in slow motion. I reached the top of the hill gasping for air but with a sense of relief and achievement. There were no medals, goody bags or t-shirts. Instead, each runner filed into the garden of the Ship Inn to be given a banana and a bottle of beer.

In the pub garden I met up with the 'photo' ladies who had all really enjoyed the event and were already talking about returning the following year. They were all staying on to enjoy the barbecue organised by the pub. It was an ideal start to the weekend, and I will look out for next year's race date, too!

The Balerno Sunday Club Run

David Syme

It's a Sunday morning, and I'm up early for breakfast. I want to have my cereal and coffee sitting comfortably inside me by the time the club run starts, at 10 am. I leave home in good time; first stop is to pick up a newspaper, then I find a good parking space at the school, our meeting point. This gives me time for a quick glance at the sports pages and my regular toilet visit, and then I'm ready. I note that the local rugby team won the previous day, and so must congratulate fellow-runner Bob, their greatest fan.

Today it all starts wrong! Most of the runners of my standard are doing a 10k race somewhere and I find myself a lone figure between the beginners and the speed merchants. I shuffle uneasily from one foot to the other, hoping for someone of my standard to arrive, but no, I'm in a peer group of one. Some of the club's stronger runners ask: "Well, Dave, how far do you want to run today?" My answer is aimed at discouraging them from joining me. "A slow hour's run would suit me today, I think."

"That's fine, Dave, we'll tag along behind you. We could do with a short slow one today after yesterday's cross-country race. Just you set the pace."

All our runs start with a sharpish climb up from the river, and I set off at a speed designed not to hold back these fast chaps. I know that I am outside my comfort zone, but I can't help it. They keep up with ease and open a conversation with me; after all, I'm not one of their regular running companions. The hill and the need to answer questions take their toll and my breathing becomes ragged. I slow down; inevitably a couple of runners deep in their own conversation cruise past me, then a few more until I am at the back of the pack. The gap between me and their back man lengthens, but at the top of the hill they are waiting for me. "OK?" They turn to go on, but I tell them to forget me from now on; I know where I am and will find my own way back. The gulf between their and my ability is so clear now that all they can say is: "Are you sure?" then off they lope.

For me the run now changes character – it improves dramatically! No longer mixing it in the fast group I can relax and choose my own route and my own pace. I may follow the agreed route or I may opt for a short cut which will give me a decent run but bring me home a little earlier. My breathing settles to a comfortable rate and before long I reach a steady speed which, were I still to have been leading the fast boys, would not have embarrassed me. It's all in the mind, I suppose…

I take a shortcut, but not the shortest option. It's still a decent run, with clear views sweeping over the Forth with the Ochill Hills on the skyline, and, behind Callander, the distant tops of Ben Vorlich and Stuc a'Chroin in the west. Feeling pleased with myself I turn for home and see far ahead of me the group of our beginners. I catch up with them slowly – they're advanced beginners – and when I reach them get into a conversation. We cover the last couple of miles with a nice chat at a gentle canter. As I am with them when we reach the car-park I join them for warm-down exercises, then drive home. While I have been running, my wife Pat has been to church, and we sit down to lunch, both well refreshed and stimulated by our morning's activity.

I have had tough Sunday club runs, easy ones, fast ones, slow ones, some in large groups, some like this one partly solo, but I've never had a bad one.

Moving Meditation aka Singing in the Rain

Eric Anderson

Eric has been running seriously since he was 16 years old. He is now 47 and has no intention of slowing down. He will tell you he is not competitive but that's a lie! He currently works as a Maritime Security Consultant specialising on counter-piracy operations. When he is on ship he stops being a 'runner' and becomes a 'skipper' as a means of keeping in shape. His preferred running environment is on the trials and mountains of his beloved Scotland.

Singing in the rain. Well, not singing but running, more like floating. Tapping out that well worn route covered in a shiny slick of water. It somehow feels softer underfoot and faster. Is it my imagination? That's how it feels to me.

We're not talking about freezing cold rain that hammers into you behind the force of a northerly wind. Oh no, we're talking about the light drizzle which soaks everything with its almost web like quality. This is the type of rain we're talking about.

Now I don't know about you but I love running in that type of rain. It has a kind of sorbothane quality. (If you don't know what that is Google it.) I especially like running in that type of rain at night. The street lights backlight it making it look like an infinite curtain of water .

When I run in these conditions I am absorbed in 'me'. The rhythm of my breathing, my heart-rate, my foot-fall…There is no splash, no impact, no shock, only horizontal movement. Time and distance mean nothing. I am running in a parallel universe. Is this 'the zone'? Everything and everybody moves around me. I don't have to check stride for anything. Magical.

During these rain-soaked runs my heart and lungs settle to an almost sedentary rate but I am flying. Flying over the ground and flying in my head. Is this the 'runners' high'? Now, I'm no Steven Tallarico (Tyler) but in his autobiography 'Does the noise inside my head bother you?' Steven describes very similar sensations whilst on Quailuuuuuuuuuuuudes man! It's also interesting that he runs, and has done for forty years, to get in shape for Aerosmith tours. Does this make me an addict? Yeah, right!

The Dali Lama doesn't run, well at least I don't think so, and he doesn't do Quailuuuuuuuuuuuudes man! Well, at least it's never been recorded. What he does do is write excellent books. These books deal with issues like living and dying – nothing heavy there then! He describes states of mind reached by meditation. He's talking about transcending through meditation. Now, I'm no expert but I do know that one requires a mantra of some sort to meditate. A phrase which is repeated in the mind to focus the mind on thinking of nothing, or something along those lines.

So, let me get back to the altered state of mind thing. Are you still with me? Ok, I've described my experience of running as moving meditation for many, many years. Now it struck me a long time ago that I have a mantra when running. This mantra was not given to me by some guru but by the simple action of running. The repetitive tapping of my feet on the ground. The power of this mantra seems to be amplified by that light drizzly rain I was writing about earlier. As water is such a powerful element this shouldn't really be a surprise to me or you for that matter. It just took some time for me to realise it. If I could only bottle it. (the energy not the water that's already been done)

So, what am I really trying to say here? An example is required methinks to illustrate the power of the 'tap, tap, tap'. Recently I spent four out of five months on various ships sailing around the

Indian Ocean. Now, these ships didn't have gyms, no treadmills, nada. The one thing I couldn't do on these ships was run. I improvised a physical training programme as best I could but no running not even to the galley for dinner. On my return I decided I would like to spend a weekend in Glencoe, get into the mountains and drink beer in the Clachaig Inn. I'm also thinking running.

Now Jimmy Saville had a cottage at the Pass of Glencoe. Why do you think that Jimmy moved there? Correct! So he could run there. I digress.

I arrive in Glencoe on a Friday, pitch my tent and get myself comfy for the coming days of clear air = clear head. Remember, I haven't run for 5 months and before that my weekly mileage was very low due to work commitments. I plan a route of about 20 miles, 30 km if you prefer, for Saturday. Fairly ambitious you might think. Saturday dawns with a perfect, and I mean perfect blue sky. There is not a cloud to be seen. I breakfast, prepare my kit and I'm off and running so to speak. I was running like an old nag right for the knackers yard. My route is taking me South along the Old Glencoe Road. The scenery is stunning which is just as well as I'm having to stop to catch my breath – ON THE FLAT! I get to my halfway point, turn and retrace my heavy steps to the campsite. I enjoyed the route but I'm a little surprised at how hard it was. I know, I know 20 miles after not running for 5 months, I know.

Now here's the crux of this story. Sunday dawns and there's a light drizzle in the air. The sort of drizzle I mentioned way back. I decide to head out on the same route as yesterday but without setting myself a distance. Dangerous game. Off I go and within five minutes I'm tapping over the ground on that cushion of water. I'm feeling good and I'm hardly breathing. I trot on and on and on. I pass the Clachaig Inn – I have a wee laugh to myself about a private joke I have with Ray Zahab about this place, Jimmy's house, The Buachaille Etive Mor and on to the Kingshouse Hotel.

I feel like I can just keep going but the sensible bit of my brain tells me that I still have to do the return journey so a quick stop at the Kingshouse and I'm on my way back. The interesting thing about the return trip is that I don't remember large sections of it. My mind was elsewhere and I don't know where that elsewhere was. A state of nothingness. Is this what transcending is all about?

Now, you are probably asking yourself where I'm going with this, right? Well, my question to myself was, 'What was different about Sunday which made the experience so much more pleasant than Saturday? And, what provided the energy for me to cover a significant distance on next to no running for 5 months?' Check out that distance on the map. Clachaig Inn to Kingshouse Hotel return then add two more miles for the run to and from the campsite.

The only difference I can see is that there was rain on Sunday. Energy giving water falling from the sky. Maybe I should email the Dali Lama and see what his take on it is – he'd probably write a book about it! Maybe I've convinced myself that rain makes me run stronger? After all, to paraphrase Ray Z, it's 90% mental and the other 10% is in your head! *

You decide!

*90% of a challenge is mental, the other 10% is in your head! (Ray Zahab, Canadian ultra-distance legend, motivational speaker, all round 'awesome' dude and my friend)

Three in One

David Syme

A family funeral took me to Conwy in North Wales. I arrived at the Castlebank Hotel mid-evening after a long drive, too tired to tackle a run right away, but keen to run early next morning. Henrique, the hotel owner, stood with me on the front step, looking over the Conwy estuary. He advised me: "Go down there all the way to the shore. A path leads you left to the marina – it's a lovely route of 2 to 3 miles." I thanked him and looked forward to a good run, if only to justify a full hotel breakfast afterwards.

I rose at six and crept out of the hotel to find a pleasant, still morning of high cloud and patches of blue sky. With the ancient town wall on my right I loped down the quiet street to the shore, turned left and settled into a steady rhythm. A coastal run invigorates at any time, but on a calm, sunny morning I felt especially good. The sea air seemed to give energy and the views were magnificent; on my right lay the exposed mud flats and calm water of the Conwy estuary with the Great Orme peninsula beyond, while a wooded hillside, alive with birdsong, rose on my left. In the distance I could soon make out a cluster of masts in the marina.

'No plan survives first contact with the enemy' is a well-known military axiom, and in my situation this morning the enemy was complacency. The run was enjoyable but too straightforward; I would reach the marina, cast an envious eye over some yachts, then run back; four or five miles on the flat. I looked for a challenge. Some way ahead and to the left I could see a wood above which lay a high ridge topped with bracken and heather. I abandoned the marina plan and headed for the hills! It did not take long to reach the foot, and I found a stile which took me over the hedge and set me off uphill. After a scramble through steep woodland (the path had disappeared just beyond the stile) I reached a tall, dense forest of ferns then emerged onto the ridge to find a well-used track. I turned away from Conwy and ran for 15 minutes up to a prominent knoll. As I had hoped, it gave fine views over the hills of Snowdonia to the west, and back over Conwy and its 13th Century castle far below to the long sweep of Colwyn Bay beyond. I gazed in all directions before taking the track east towards the town. If the coast is invigorating, how about an early morning run along a ridge high above a sleepy town! I continued past my ascent route and dropped gently to the first houses. Before long I saw the dark grey stones of the town wall which signalled the end of my run, which had taken just over one hour. Breakfast did not start until 8.30, I was in no hurry, so I went past the hotel into the town. I was surprised to find that access to the wall ramparts was open, so I went to the far end and climbed the spiral staircase. I found that I could run over the smooth stone and did so, much to the indignation of resident seagulls, who were not used to early morning runners and made their objection loud and clear. There are only two sides to the town wall still standing, but they gave me great views both inland and out to the estuary, also down into the narrow streets of the town itself. Helpful notices told me of the town's history and warned me not to do any off-piste climbing on the crumbling watchtowers. Running by the sea and running along a ridge are all very well, but running alone along three-quarters of a mile of a World Heritage Inscribed Site is also a great experience!

I pattered down the steps at the end of the wall and jogged back to the hotel, passing dozy schoolchildren at a bus stop who gazed at me in mild curiosity. As I climbed the steps to the hotel door I felt triumphant; my run had had three distinctly different phases, each offering me a particular pleasure. When did I last enjoy such a rich three-in-one run?

Now, what's for breakfast…

The Running Joke

David Syme

It happened as we approached the end of an 8-mile Sunday morning club run near Balerno.

We had set off as a group of twelve or so, but the group had splintered at a couple of points and now there were just four of us heading for home. The weather had been 'character-building'. The paths at Harlaw had been muddy and slippery, the country roads awash with rain and flood water, and for much of our run we had been buffeted by a strong headwind. The four of us were running along a quiet, straight stretch of road, and, to break the tedium, I started telling a joke.

"This woman from up north decided to spend her 50th birthday on a weekend in London." I started, and the group drew closer together. "She booked into a smart hotel, then went shopping. In the evening she went to a musical, then she went to the hotel for bed. The next morning she asked for the bill, and was horrified to be asked to pay £270. She demanded to see the manager."

There was a pause as we broke into single file to let a car pass.

"This is ridiculous! £270 for 1 night? I was only in the hotel for 8 hours – I'm not paying that much!" The manager said: "Madam, we have three cocktail bars and two restaurants."

"But I didn't use them," she replied.

"No," came the response, "but you could have. We also have a fitness centre with spa, gymnasium and swimming pool."

"I never went near these places!" retorted the northerner.

"No, but you could have." Came the smooth reply. Our lady went to the counter, wrote a cheque and gave it to the manager. "But this is only for £70," he spluttered. "Your room costs £270"

The group sensed the punch-line and strained to catch it…

"I've charged you £200 for sleeping with me." "But I didn't sleep with you!" "No, but you could…"

The last word of this punch-line was lost as K, who was running on my right shoulder, fell headlong onto the road. When striding onto the edge of a puddle she was unfortunate enough to have put her right foot into a deep pot-hole. She lay for a moment in the wet, then, with our help, gingerly stood up. She had clearly damaged her ankle, and was suffering from shock. She was also miffed to note a hole in a glove and a tear in her training pants. After a minute or so she felt able to put some weight onto the foot, the ankle of which was already swelling up, and together we limped the mile or so back until she was picked up and taken home. Later it was confirmed that she had suffered a bad ankle strain, with a broken finger into the bargain.

It could have been worse, but I wonder if I had contributed to her accident by drawing her concentration from the road? Perhaps she would have run behind me and avoided the puddle, had she not wanted to hear the end of the joke? Should I have steered a line to let her avoid the puddle? My 'punishment' for (perhaps) distracting K was that no-one had laughed at the joke. Even when we were able to relax after the immediate shock it didn't feel right to return to it, although I wanted to know if they had enjoyed it. I remembered the alleged question put to Mary Lincoln in 1865 in the Ford Theatre in Washington by the manager, just after husband Abe had been assassinated: "Apart from this, Mrs Lincoln, did you enjoy the show?" … and held my tongue.

The Water of Leith

David Syme

The Water of Leith is described as 'a silver thread in a green ribbon'. It is a small river which flows south-west to north-east through Edinburgh. It is twenty-four miles in length, the lower half having a popular walkway which offers to a runner a route full of diversity and charm. It has a special appeal to me. In the 50s I went to school at John Watson's, now the Gallery of Modern Art, which overlooks the river. (Five decades later the river has the same distinctive smell which takes me right back to my teens as I pass below the building.) I worked in a warehouse near the river-mouth in Leith in my student days, and have spent most of my life following Scottish rugby at Murrayfield. (How often did we cross that river in confident expectation, then 2 hours later in triumph or in disappointment?) In the 80s and 90s I crossed the river at Slateford and climbed the Dell on my daily running or cycling commute to work as a schoolteacher in Colinton. Nowadays I join my Harmeny club-mates for runs from Balerno, many of which start or end with a section along the river. It is a route full of memories; join me on a run from Balerno to Leith....

The first section is close to the river, along the track of the old Caledonian Railway's Balerno Loop. Up until 1949 trains could leave the main Edinburgh to Carstairs or Glasgow lines at Slateford and rejoin them at Camps. Now the track is popular with cyclists, pram-pushers and dog-walkers here, so as we set off we do a bit of dodging and weaving, always with a friendly greeting. Jogging down the steep-sided leafy path we see old railway cuttings with stone revetments, where the great Currie-born mountaineer Dougal Haston had his first taste of rock climbing. Mills for the manufacture of textiles, paper and snuff used to line the river, now they are either derelict or have been made into housing – there's plenty to see as we settle into an easy rhythm along the flat track just below and to the east of the A70, one of the radial approaches to Edinburgh's centre. The first landmark is the city bypass, high above on a modern bridge. Walkway signposts here tell us how far we have gone and how far to go, but these contradict themselves in places, so we won't take them too seriously! The valley widens as we approach Colinton; we give a sad 'tut-tut' as we pass the offices of Scotland's much-missed airline Globespan, which went into receivership because of unpaid bills. Soon we are running under the Gillespie Road bridge at the foot of Colinton Village and entering the railway tunnel. I'm told it is known as Henry's Tunnel, based on Thomas the Tank Engine lore. Thankfully it is only a few hundred metres long and is well-lit, and then we emerge into the daylight of the Dell. This is one of the wilderness natural parks in Edinburgh, its densely-wooded slopes criss-crossed with paths. Still on the old railway line, we keep our height on the western bank for a short distance, then plunge downhill to cross the river and continue on the eastern side. We pass a small stone belvedere (could be useful if it starts to pour!) and are soon encountering traffic for the first time when we emerge onto Lanark Road, near a pub.

We cross the road and pass the Water of Leith Visitor Centre, which, if we haven't been seduced by the pub's offerings, could tempt us with its tea and home baking. We are now close to the water, and the wooded valley has given way to urban features and flat terrain. We pass a cemetery and allotments, look over to Saughton Prison, then come to a second traffic radial, Gorgie Road. (On one run I was seduced here, not by a pub or cafe, but by the butcher shop of John Bain at Stenhouse Cross, where the juicy mince pies are something else! End of that run…) We cross this road and continue down the east bank to Saughton Park, often bustling with youthful soccer matches. Leaving the park, we cross Balgreen Road and are back along the river bank. The pulse beats a little quicker as we approach our national rugby stadium. Through iron bars we might see the national team training on the back pitches as we pass. This section is highly popular with dog-walkers, so we must keep one wary eye on the path as well as looking at or for the rugby players… We go round the ice rink, past parkland where in summer a game of cricket might be played, then cross the busy road at Roseburn. Now we descend under a bridge of another former railway line to the peace of parkland again. What's this? We have run into 'Gormley-land'. The famous sculptor has erected 6 life-size metal statues in or near the river – remember the diversity and charm I mentioned at the beginning? Here we run below the Modern Art Gallery. As schoolboys we were convinced that a WW2 bomb had dropped into the river just above the weir, creating a deep hole where monster trout lurked. As we never caught anything over 1lb it remained merely a legend. The path now hugs the east bank, then crosses just before Belford Bridge. We are back to steep wooded slopes, but the opposite bank has the crowded buildings of fashionable Dean Village. We must be careful on the next section; if the water is high it may be tricky where the path goes right down to the water's edge. I had to climb a 2 metre wall once to continue my run with dry feet. A bit of twisting and turning under the towering Dean Bridge and we are trotting towards Stockbridge. I am not too fond of this section to Cannonmills. It is a bewildering stretch where we seem to change direction frequently, only regaining a straight line to Leith at Warriston. It is on this section, however, that friends and I saw a kingfisher once. If we see one today, its brilliant blue flashing over the dirty grey water and green reeds will lift the spirits! Tired legs will be also revived when we pass under Great Junction Street, as it marks the start of the home straight. The river has been reasonably clean up to now but as it widens it picks up the detritus of the industrial, commercial and social aspects of Leith. Never mind, we're nearly there! For me there is no Finish Line to this run. The warehouse of my student days 'SPD' (Speedy Prompt Deliveries aka Slavery Pays Dividends) is long gone, and the efforts of the 12 miles have rendered our perspiring bodies unwelcome in pub or cafe. No, it's on with the spare tops we have carried and straight to the bus stop on Bernard Street where we can catch the first of two buses which will take us all the way back to Balerno and the car. It is a shame not to celebrate a great run in one or more of the pubs for which Leith is justly famous, but a shower and a change of clothes come first.

It's less than a half marathon, but we see so much and have many stop-start points that it seems longer. If you fancy a run with a difference, come on! Step down to the silver thread on the green ribbon!

Running made Simple

David McKendrick

Can you believe that there are people out there who think that running is simple? Can you? In their deluded world they think that 'good' runners simply run faster, or for longer, or in more trying circumstances. These people's simplicity is incredible. Wee men in white coats will soon turn up, put them in the back of a van and take them away to a re-education camp. Here they will learn some, or all of what follows. For some they might even learn more.

Running is far from simple. It takes organisation, commitment and if you want to achieve anything – no little dedication. The average runner you see in the street plodding through the rain / hail / shine (well mostly rain) will not simply have thought to themselves, "I know I'll nip out for a quick run!" it simply does not happen like that.

There are a whole series of considerations. Firstly, the time factor. Most runners do not have the luxury of lots of times to plan their runs. Some might have developed some kind of protected time when they can go out but for many finding the time is the first in a series of problems. We runners live in dread of our nearest and dearest announcing the intention to go out for the day. Such announcements are met with a quickening sense of dread, "Oh, no," we think, "I had a ten miler planned," such requests are usually discouraged in the sure and certain knowledge that you will incur the wrath of the aforementioned nearest and dearest. But what can you do? After all you need to run.

Presuming you manage to get the time to do it there is then the question of the route. Runners are masochists. A nice flat run over a relatively short distance? Nope. For me I have to run up a hill, the bigger the better, if I don't hear the sound of the blood pumping in my ears then I don't feel I have done enough. Distance is only a part of it. There needs to be variety and most importantly there needs to be a challenge.

So assuming you have the time bit sorted out (who cares if you are in the dog house?) and a route you are happy with (Well, you are never really happy, every route can be improved) you then have the issue of the gear. Running introduces you to a whole new vocabulary; how many non-runners know what wicking is? Not many I bet, but we all do. Or socks, do you wear those traditional white ones or go for the trainer sock? And now they come in many colours; so many that even Americans comment on them! Never mind the whole issue of the trainers, ACIS, New Balance, Adidas (Gabresellaise wears Adidas) it's all so confusing.

But wait help is at hand! *Runners World*, a magazine for all of us, we get antsy waiting on it coming in; there is always something in it for us. The internet has been a godsend for us. We can obsess on line! We can tweet, skype and facebook, the possibilities are boundless. I follow Mo Farah on Twitter, just in case he ever wants my opinion on trainer socks!

The truth is as well as offering us the opportunity to improve our health to get and stay fit and to push our own boundaries, running allows us to be healthily obsessed (get it? 'healthily' obsessed) It provides a focus, allows us to be in control. For me in a life that is controlled by work and finances and families, running is mine, it's for me and I love it.

Runners are generally nice to other runners. I have a friend who is much better than me but he will regularly offer to go out with me for a run. As soon as I say no he tells me not too worry he will go at my pace. Frankly I think he would kill me if he had to run at my pace but the offer is there, even if I will never take it up. Some runners join running clubs that become as much about the social side as anything else. For some they can develop their own abilities and become coaches, helping others achieve their potential.

Inside every runner is an obsessive. We know this, and that is why we are nice to each other, we are all members of the same wee club. We share the same nerdiness and we actually quite like it, you should try it, it's fun.

So, non-runners, that was an insight into the world we live in, it's quite nice, there are sacrifices but they all become worth it if you achieve your goals. A Personal Best in a 10k provides a welcome glow, you know all the hassle was worth it. You have proved something.

So you non runners – next time you see someone out running and you think they look exhausted just remember the effort it took for them to get there. Even better come out and try it for yourself.

Snippets

Registration

On Sunday I went for a run with the club. I set off with a group of strong runners and held my own. I found myself running alongside lean, fit runners whose exploits in races far exceed my own. I felt good. There was a spring in my step. When we returned to the car-park after 8 miles I was fresh – could have gone on. I drove home in buoyant mood.

On Monday I registered for a marathon.

I turned up for the club run on Wednesday evening. As I warmed up I felt a twinge in my left calf, so stretched it carefully. We set off uphill and almost immediately my breathing became laboured. My calf began to protest, and I could hear my feet thud-thudding as my running style deteriorated to a pathetic shamble. After 3 miles I gasped an excuse and turned for home.

It's all in the mind!

Don't!

You are on a solo run and feel tired.
If you have to slow to a walk, check frequently to front and rear for

other runners. You must **not** be seen walking by fellow runners. Seeing you walking in running kit they will throw you a pitying look which will haunt you for days.

You are going for a run with the club.
Wear a neutral T-shirt, or one from a modest 10k race. Wearing the marathon shirt from the days when you could do these things (but no longer can) marks you down as a has-been wannabe.

You are in a race and can't work out your kilometre per minute times.
Your ability to do mental arithmetic is lost after the first km. Don't worry, this is normal. Write down your times on a piece of paper if you must, but on no account ask fellow runners. They will take you for an idiot.

You are out for a run and you see a runner coming towards you.
In the country give a greeting, which can vary from a comment "You're going well!" to a brief wave of the hand. In the city do **not** greet the runner, or he/she will take you for a weirdo.

The Bitch in the Park

I was running through the Almondell Park near Livingston, my thoughts miles away when…

"Leave that runner alone, Judy!" A stout lady whooped, as her spaniel repeatedly leapt up at me, yapping enthusiastically. "She loves to play," the lady added gleefully, looking around to see if any other park users were also enjoying the spectacle of me in a Michael Jackson dance routine as I avoided contact with the playful Judy.

"What fun!" I hissed through clenched teeth, as I escaped

and worked my way through the gears back to my cruising speed. Still, I thought a few minutes later, it was not all bad. Instead of instructing Judy not to harass the elderly, overweight jogger, she had called me 'a runner'.

Greeting

Scottish summer
Hot weekend
Solo jogger
Pasture land
Haiku!

How about a Special Run today?

Colin McPhail

Colin is the proprietor of Footworks Running Shop in Bruntsfield Place, Edinburgh and a passionate runner. Every Sunday morning at 9.30 am a group of runners meets at the shop for their weekly dose of oxygen and endorphins. They vary in age, ability, speed and endurance, so when they turn up they have no idea what they are letting themselves in for! The group also selects particular races in the year and helps members to set their individual targets and meet them.

Colin with wife, Isla and daughter, Sally

As is usual on a Sunday morning I turned up for the group run, but on this Sunday in early November of 2011 I had a cunning plan. The British Heart Foundation was holding 5k and 10k races at 11 am in Holyrood Park. I addressed the group: "Why don't we run down to the park, enter the 10k race and then run back up here again? It would give us 10–12 miles with a race in the middle!" The response was varied, but overall negative. Some had no money with them, others baulked at the idea of paying £15 just to run twice round a park they knew well. Perhaps I should have floated my idea the previous week…?

I shrugged and we set off for Blackford Hill, a favourite run with some of Edinburgh's finest streets, the well-kept grounds of Ashley Ainslie Hospital with a steep climb onto the hill itself. On the top you can have spectacular views in good weather – east as far as May Island, north to the Lomond Hills and Benarty Hill and west as far as Ben Lomond. No wonder they built the Royal Observatory on this hill! We turned west towards the Braid Hills, descending steeply to the Braid Burn and crossing it on the Dean Haugh path which offers a heart-pounding climb to the top. My 'claret-loading' of the night before was reminding me that perhaps 'carbo-loading' makes more sense.

Waiting for the group to re-form on the top gave us a chance to admire more great views, then we turned west and dropped down to the golf course heading for Frogston Road and a more urban route. Liberton Brae is a devil to run up, but a delight to run down, and we enjoyed the long lope all the way to Cameron Toll. With 8 miles behind us, most of the group had 'forked off' by now, leaving me with one other chap, Chris. We decided to go and take a look at the 10k race, perhaps cheer in the winners, make a donation. Both of us were wearing barefoot-style shoes, which are designed to make us stronger runners over time. They take some getting used to, and Chris was wearing his for only the second time. We reached the Start desk at 11.15, where the marshals looked at our running kit and tried unsuccessfully to mask their look of: "Ye missed the 11 o'clock start, ya pair of plonkers!" I offered a donation to the girl at Registration, and she accepted it, but said that we "may as well race even though it started nearly 20 minutes ago." She handed us numbers and timing chips and asked: "10k or 5k?"

I gave Chris a long look… he shook his head and said, "You've got to be joking!"

"It's only 10k," I chirped, not mentioning that it would be more than 18 miles when we got back to the shop, 6.2 against the clock!

It was 25 minutes after the official start when we crossed the line and made our way up the road to Dunsapie Loch. We stuck together, resisting the temptation to chase the front runners who began to overtake us. The charming marshals at the water station apologised at the lack of champagne so we settled for water. Chris was suffering in his barefoot shoes and opted to stop after the first lap, giving himself a 5k time. I charged down the hill and then slowed down to start the second 5 k lap. Mark Cooper (24 hours in a Glasgow Bar) was finishing his 10k as he tapped me on the shoulder and wished me a pleasant second lap. I caught up with and overtook some of the back markers, and this gave me some self-respect and the incentive to race to the Finish. Once more up at the loch water station the lady marshal had no clear explanation for the lack of champagne, so it had to be water again. By this stage the strike of the barefoot shoes was exerting an influence on my feet. With no orthotics and no support my medial ankle joints were giving me gyp and telling me that the 5k would have been far enough (well done, Chris!). Well, hey ho… there's only one thing to do once you've started, so I kept going and dug into my reserves until I could enjoy the soft grass on the long down slope to the Finish, where I crossed in the sprint/crawl of a runner who has given his all. Another race bites the dust! The girl at Registration congratulated me: "Told you you wouldn't be last!"

With medals round our necks Chris and I ran the 2 miles back to the shop, aware that we had overdone the Sunday run in barefoot shoes*, but with only some discomfort as a result.

Next year I will give early notice of this event and we'll put it in our race calendar. With luck we'll have a monster entry. It's well-organised by friendly folk, and it is for a very good cause.

I wonder if they'll have any champagne next year?

*Colin is keen to promote minimalist running shoes. See his barefoot debate page at www.facebook.com/barefootworks or email him at colinmcphail@marathonrunning.co.uk

'Some of One and a Lot of the Other'

Andrew Syme

One of the advantages of a home run is that you know exactly what's in store for you. A short flat one… hilly… long… wind-exposed… rural… urban etc, so a decision can be made depending on weather, fitness level or purpose of the run. Living in the Alps in Garmisch-Partenkirchen I'm so spoilt for choice; sometimes it's difficult to decide!

Two years ago in the spring I made the decision to run up to a hut which is situated about a third of the way up a mountain called the Kramer. I thought I knew exactly what was in store for me but I was in for a surprise!

This is a favourite route of mine especially in spring because, although it's quite steep it only goes up from 750m in the valley to about 1100m, so by April it's normally snow-free. The run starts off on a road which I soon leave, turning onto a lovely well-kept path which contours around the mountain. After a few kilometres the path divides and I then start the steep climb to the St Martin Hut. On this occasion I was surprised to see quite a few walkers around, some of them even stopped and started clapping! I thought they were only complimenting me on my running style but this happened two or three times and, as nobody has ever clapped my running style before, I became suspicious. I kept on running, the walkers and clappers became more numerous until before I had grasped the situation I was cheered over a Finish line at the Hut. I'd accidentally run up a race route! I was soon surrounded by people congratulating me on winning so as soon as I got my breath back I started explaining that I was not in the race. The crowds quickly lost interest in me so I then jogged back down the hill, cheering on the first racers as they battled their way up the hill.

I later found out the race was a memorial run in remembrance of a young local athlete who died in a rock climbing accident several years before.

The next year I became involved with the same race but in a totally different way. Racers only take part by invitation, and I had been invited. It was a 6 pm start quite close to home so I told my wife I should be back by 8 pm – big mistake. Thirty runners were invited, a mix of runners, rock climbers and mountain climbers most of whom I knew. Rucksacks were handed in, start numbers written on palms and last course info given out before the start. The race itself was fairly uneventful, hard work with the last steep climb to the Finish line. I expected a quick chat with the other runners, a shaking of hands etc then the run back down home, how wrong I was! We all piled into the hut and made ourselves comfortable around the large wooden tables. Looking around I realised how traditional and cosy this hut is. Everything is in wood, a low roof gives it that cosy feeling, with pictures of barrel-chested Bavarian chaps with folded arms and smoking long pipes looking down on us. A women in the traditional Dirndl dress serving beers completed the perfect hut atmosphere. Before I knew it huge 2 litre (approx 4 pints) glasses filled with the frothy local yeast beer appeared on our table. These were promptly passed around with everyone taking several large gulps. The organiser then did a short presentation, thanking everyone for coming. He also introduced the parents of the deceased lad, They had had the idea of sponsoring this race each year in honour of their son. Their thinking was that their son would have enjoyed such an evening and that it should be a happy occasion. There then followed a minute's silence.

The prize-giving started; there was no absolute winner but instead they pulled numbers out of the hat to form teams of two, added the times together with the shortest combined time winning. After a while my name was called out so up I went to the prize-giving table with my team mate. First we were both handed €5, then we were invited to take a swig of sparkling wine from a large silver mug before being told to choose a prize from the table. I picked up a runner's head torch then returned to my seat. The evening sped away, more beers appeared, and it got warm and steamy in the hut as the air outside rapidly cooled. At about 11 pm the buxom waitress told us "That's it for tonight." So jackets and woolly hats were donned and out we went into the crisp night air. It was only then that I realised I was fairly unsteady on my feet and I was not the only one. With head torches on all 30 of us started the long trudge down, enjoying occasional glimpses of the lights of Garmisch through the trees. Some songs were sung to which I, to my frustration, couldn't contribute, so I started singing ' Flower of Scotland' which hardly surprisingly ended up being a rather embarrassing solo effort. I eventually got home with glowing cheeks, a grin on my face and smelling strongly of beer and met the wrath of my wife. She asked me if I'd been running or drinking so I replied:" Some of one and a lot of the other."

Every Runner Has His Day

David Syme

It was my home 10k, so I knew the course well. At the start there were many local runners, so greetings and good wishes were exchanged, but I always had an eye for other runners who looked to be in my age group. There were four definites, and I noted that they were eyeing me up, too!

We were off at a gallop but soon slowed to a more suitable pace. I settled in behind two of my rivals, who were running together. I knew that a third was behind us, and had lost the fourth. Together the three of us began to work our way through the field. The course is described as 'undulating' – most racers know to interpret this as 'hilly'. I knew where there were ups and downs, and planned my race. At 4k there is a steep up-slope which goes on and on. Just as we started climbing I eased alongside the two and then changed up a gear in a controlled overtaking manoeuvre. They did not respond, but I kept the speed up until I reached the down slope beyond the wood. Expecting a counter attack I opened my stride and loped down fairly quickly. Adrenalin was now flowing and I felt great! I was able to overtake several groups of runners and could see that the racers were thinning out. For one who normally races at the back end of the pack this was a new experience! My breathing and legs seemed happy at this fast cruise, so I kept it up, and saw the fourth rival ahead – a slim, short chap with his head to one side and a rhythmic, stabbing pace. I knew that I would catch up with him on the next hill, so slowed slightly to go at his speed, just behind him. As we started the uphill stretch I did the same as before, cruising past him without a sideward glance, attacking the hill and loving it! At the brow I glanced behind to see where he was, but he was nowhere to be seen. "That's it!" I said to myself, "I've a good chance to be up there in my age group." The thought gave me wings, and I was able to maintain my overtaking speed until 8k, passing several runners in the process. Just after the 8k marker I saw a friend with his dog.

"Well done, Dave," he shouted, "you're ninth!"

"Ninth!" I thought. That means that I am performing far above my usual level. The highest position I have held in this race is 57th, 3rd in my age group! Perhaps I should slow down a bit…? I asked my body, and the first parts of me to reply were my eyes. Look, they told me, there are three just ahead, you could be sixth! The eyes had it, and off I went, reeling in the three who were beginning to struggle. Seeing an old runner like me steaming past must really have knocked the stuffing out of them! And still I felt good! With 1k to go I saw two ahead, and two just in front of them. Could I…? Yes I could! I was on cruise control and feeling great. I had never been like this in a race before, and I was loving it. One of the two chaps ahead was a top runner from my club. Could I really be coming alongside…passing him? Yes I could, and – to his credit – he got over his surprise quickly enough to wish me well. Over the last 1k there were spectators, some of whom knew me and encouraged me wildly. "You are 2nd, Dave!" They shouted, and, when I passed my friend Jim he yelled: "Go on, Dave, the leader looks shattered!" I saw him ahead, but he didn't look shattered. It took a supreme effort, but I caught up with him as we came to the final hill. He had thought himself to be well clear and so sprinted forward in shock when I appeared on his shoulder. Some of me responded by saying – OK you've done well today, don't be over-ambitious, 2nd is a great result…. but another voice inside told me that today was my day. That chap might win a race tomorrow, or next month, but today was my day. I focussed on the broad red FINISH banner and drove towards it. I caught up with him with 100m to go. For some time we ran neck and neck, but then he faded. He fell away behind and I was over the line as the winner. I stopped with quivering legs and heaving chest. Astonished friends and club-mates gathered round enthusiastically and thumped my back vigorously.

One particular thump was accompanied by the words: "Wake up! You have to be at the dentist's at eight-fifteen!"

AWAY

Time Pressure

David Syme

I was teaching on a course at the Swiss Military Academy at Birmensdorf, near Zurich.

"Do you see the towers on top of that hill on the hill over there?" asked Halm, a young militia man doing his annual camp at Birmensdorf. "That's the Uetliberg, it's 869m high. There's a railway right to the top. When you get there, you climb the smaller tower to a viewing platform. There are great views over Zurich and the lake. Lots of tourists go for the view – you see people from all over the world up there. I ran there recently – it took me 2 hours there and back."

It was nearly 5 pm and I was just leaving the Academy to change and go for a run, but was aware that they stopped serving the evening meal punctually at 7 pm, so a 2 hour run to the towers was out of the question, but.... Uetliberg lay in a direction I had not yet explored, so I set off at 5.10pm with the intention of checking out the first half of the route for a possible crack at it later.

Birmensdorf lies in a dip, 440m above sea level, so all routes lead uphill. Today's one took me up quiet tarmac roads until I joined the busy main road to Zurich. It was hard work and after a long slog up the pavement I was glad to slip off to the right at Waldegg onto a path through a pine wood. A glance at my watch surprised me; only 25 minutes gone! I could perhaps make a stab

99

at the summit after all. I decided that my turn-back time would be 6 pm. Assuming that I would be faster by 10 minutes on the downhill way back, that would give me 20 minutes to shower and meet the 7 pm deadline, smelling sweetly and in respectable clothes.

There was now a touch of urgency in my step, and that is my excuse for missing the track I should have been on. Instead I found myself on a broad track heading rapidly downhill towards Zurich, so I turned right and plunged uphill into the forest in a direct line to the summit. In between the trees the foresters had left fallen branches, bramble thickets and clumps of bushes in natural regeneration, so progress was slow, indeed delicate in places. Eventually I reached another track, but it too seemed to be too gentle, so I continued my fall-line climb, until I came to the railway track. Now I knew that it led to the summit, so that was good news, as was the sight of the towers above me. It was 5.59, but I was so close that I was definitely going to reach the top, however long it took. I ran beside the rails until I met a crossing, followed the road a couple of hundred metres, then sprinted (yes!) up the last line of steps to the summit ridge. It was 6.09. I peeped at the dramatic view, took some foliage and seed pods out of my socks and laces then headed down again at 6.11

The next 20 minutes were wonderful as I flew down a pleasant road on the wings of hunger. I had a sporting chance of reaching my room and making it for supper before the metal roller curtain would be pulled down at the serving hatch on the dot of 7. Another plus was that I found a much quicker route down with no 'off-piste' sections. At Ringlikon Station a map board showed me that running through the village would cut off much of the unpleasant main road, so I trotted down the quiet street. I am never a stylish runner, but a passer-by would have noted a shambling urgency in my legs and a grim determination on my face. That passer-by might have guessed that my doctor had told me to run and I hated every step, or I had left my wallet in a pub 10 miles back down the road and was anxious to find it before anyone else did.

Ringlikon is a very fashionable dormitory village and there were, in fact, no passers-by, only some exotic whiffs of haute cuisine from kitchen windows. When I reached the main road I looked at my watch again – 6.35! The rest of the route was steep descent on tarmac, and I made good time, reaching the barracks at 6.47 exactly.

Then a funny thing happened. I decided not to dash to the shower, fling on street clothes and dash to the canteen, arriving triumphantly at 6.59. I walked calmly straight to the canteen foyer and picked up two bananas and an orange. One of the canteen staff told me to grab a tray and take a meal just as I was – no-one would mind my unkempt state at all. "No," I said loftily, "I'm trying to lose a kilo or two. This fruit will be fine, but make sure you have a big bowl for my breakfast muesli tomorrow morning."

7th Annual Pat's Run

Paul Houston

Paul lives in Edinburgh and is a leading member of Harmeny Pentland Runners with a passion for ultras in USA.

After my trip to Las Vegas for the Labor of Love 100-mile race, I travelled down to Arizona for some exploring and much needed swimming pool time. Having spent a great day in the snow at Flagstaff, I got up early for the drive down to Phoenix and overheard the words '4.2 mile road race' and '24,000 runners' on the TV news. Although I was still in quite a bit of discomfort from the 100 mile race, I had to find out more. When I heard the full story, I was sold. The race was taking place three days later in Phoenix. It was called 'Pat's Run' and, although quite pricey, all proceeds went to the Pat Tillman foundation. I looked further into the background of the charity, and raced down to Phoenix to get my last-minute entry in.

The foundation provides support to active and ex-US servicemen, particularly in relation to education. It was set up in honour of Pat Tillman. Pat's story is tragic. He was an exceptional American football player who started his professional sporting career at Arizona State University, where the race is now run. He then went on to play in the NFL for the Arizona Cardinals. Following the 9/11 attacks of 2001, Pat turned down a $3 million footballing contract to enlist in the US army. He went on to serve several tours including some in Iraq and Afghanistan. Two years after initially enlisting, Pat was tragically killed in Afghanistan by friendly fire. To honour his memory the Pat Tillman foundation was set up and 'Pat's race' became an annual tradition, supported by the whole of the Phoenix valley community. To have 24,000+ people enter a 4.2 mile race shows the high regard in which Pat Tillman and the foundation are held. So I entered as soon as I arrived in Phoenix and resolved just to enjoy the event without worrying about times and pace. I would just run how I felt. This allowed me to enjoy my last night in the US by having a few drinks in a local bar, knowing that I didn't have to worry about not being in top form the next day.

The morning of the race was pretty much as expected. The race started at 7 am so I was up at 5 am after 5 hours of sleep. As soon as I arrived at the race staging area though, the atmosphere dispelled the remaining tiredness. There was a real carnival feeling with thousands of people walking around, warming up and chatting excitedly. At 6.55 am the national anthem was played live by trumpet musician, Jesse McGuire. Although not a US citizen, the hairs on the back of my neck stood up when he hit the high note towards the end of the anthem and the whole crowd cheered manically. In fact, the emotion of the music and the event almost got the better of me! The rendition fired everyone up…and then we were off. Despite a conservative estimated finishing time, I was still put in the first pen along with the super athletic-looking college runners. I sneaked to the very back of the pen to avoid holding anyone up. Luckily, starting up front gave us all a relatively fast and clear start. I quickly settled into a 6:40-ish pace with the bunch.

People who know me, know of my huge love for Arizona. Tempe in particular is a beautiful up-and-coming city district with a huge lake and series of bridges crossing the water. Half a mile in, we made a right turn and headed over the bridge. In the mild temperatures under clear blue skies, a huge smile came across my face. I was just so happy to be there at that precise moment.

This carried me along and my pace crept up. After 2 miles, I was still feeling comfortable. I had a quad niggle from the 100 miler that I could feel very slightly but it was definitely improving day by day and it didn't bother me at all. The great thing about this race, is that it is all about community. Everyone comes together to support the race and everyone can take part, whether running or walking the entire route. This really hit home after a couple of miles. There were all shapes and sizes enjoying the day and lots of supporters lining the route cheering all runners and offering supportive words.

With less than a mile to go, the pace had increased to 6:00 m/m but it was still comfortable. We arrived back at the starting area and ran parallel to the starting funnel. We were a couple of

Paul with cheerleaders after the race.

minutes from finishing the race and there were still thousands of people waiting to start! We were hit with a wall of cheering from everyone still waiting to start and with half a mile to go, I went for it!

One of the big draws of the race for me, apart of course from the very deserving charity, was the fact that the race finished on the 42 yard line of the Sun Devil Stadium, the ASU football field where Pat Tillman used to play. We ran up a slight hill to the stadium and straight onto the field. A few hundred spectators had made their way into the stadium and were cheering us home. Still feeling good, I put everything into finishing as hard as possible and crossed the line in 26:06. Not my fastest time by some way, but with fatigued legs, I was delighted that they held up.

Just when I thought the race couldn't get any better, I was greeted at the end by three Arizona State University cheerleaders and got a hug and great picture as a souvenir of a truly memorable race.

Run for your Beds!

Jonathan Wyatt

Traveling from New Zealand and spending 4 months each year in Europe has always been a big adventure for me. I have been a distance runner, racing a lot in track and field but I've always enjoyed the sense of the unexpected you get by not really knowing where you are going and the surprises you can happen upon when travelling, running and racing.

My first visit to Europe was far from straightforward. For a track runner trying to run personal best times and stay in peak fitness, it was tough travelling by myself to a big city and trying to find a place to stay or eat. It was tough negotiating with the race meeting director to give me a place on the start line. Most of the elite athletes at these races had their own manager but I was not quite in that league. I would backpack my way around Europe taking in the architecture and history while also training as hard as I could. My racing times over 3, 5 and 10,000m were good, and being from a different country often helped get me those elusive starts because then the race could say they had a more international field with a New Zealander there. But half the time they wouldn't put me in the field, and it was tough trying to peak for a top performance in a race not knowing if I would even be able to start.

So after wondering if I was tough enough to do it all over again a year later, following a particularly long stint in Europe for track racing, I accepted an invitation from two of my friends from New Zealand, Aaron and Megan, to travel with them in a Euro-leased Renault around the mountains of Europe – running.

From this first ever season of Mountain Running I have some of my favourite running memories. Until this point I was a road runner and a track runner although cross country races were arguably my strongest discipline. But I took to running up mountains pretty well as it suited my ability to keep moving fast over a long period of time and suffering the burn of the long uphill climbs. I also loved the freedom of running in nature, usually in some spectacular alpine scenery. We teamed up with Paul from Australia and the four of us set about exploring a new race every weekend in the Bavarian, Swiss, Austrian, French and Italian alps.

We arrived in Zermatt, Switzerland late on a summer evening after a long drive from Briancon in France, passing through Chamonix and descending into the Swiss Canton of Valais. We had started the journey late, not realising that our French hosts in Briancon would not let us say farewell until we had finished a leisurely lunch. This was lovely but left us in a bit of a hurry to reach the tourist office in Zermatt before it closed.

In France you drive like the French, so enjoy the general freedom to overtake where you think it's possible, but on reaching Switzerland we were more nervous. We had heard that the local traffic police could issue a ticket and take payment on the spot by credit card. But the mountain roads were quickly dispatched by our driver Aaron and we arrived in time, although a little subdued, our stomachs not feeling quite the 100% they were when we finished our French lunch.

We met the race organizer and listened vaguely to the arrangements. We were told to take a room at a hotel in this alpine ski resort town and, since we were invited runners, the race organizer was providing our accommodation. Great! We had a good night's sleep and were all ready to set off on the race the next day.

Race morning was a beautiful morning with clear, crisp air and a view up to the Matterhorn, which forms a backdrop to this town that also attracts an incredible number of tourists. We walked to the starting area (since cars are forbidden in Zermatt although the silent electric lorries and mini cars are probably just as deadly to pedestrians) and picked up our start numbers. But on arriving we were informed that our provided accommodation only ran to one night and that we had just used it up so to stay the additional night which we would need in order to stay for the race and ceremony would cost us something in the region of 230 Swiss francs each per night. This was something of a shock, for all our budgeting until that point had consisted of hostel accommodation, and we ran a pretty tight ship by cooking our own food and staying with local people we met whenever we could. However, we were given a glimmer of hope when the race organizer did mention that some of the finer local hotels were offering age group prizes of hotel vouchers for accommodation and that if we were all able to win or arrive in the top three of our respective categories we might be out of this awkward situation.

The Matterhornlauf mountain race is one of the really beautiful mountain runs. It climbs from the town of Zermatt at 1620m up to the Scharzsee at 2583m. We ran on alpine paths, crossing flower-filled meadows, leaping snow-melt streams and steep rocky slopes with the Matterhorn always towering over us. But of course we were all concentrating on having a good race that day! When we ran the course we ran with some extra motivation. We were inspired by the mountains and the natural scenery and then we were inspired to run fast so that we would have a place to sleep that night!

On finishing at the top of the Scharzsee we lined up the envelope vouchers we had won over a plate of Kaiserschmarrn (an energy replenishing pancake and apple combination) and a glass of Weissbier. Would this be an expensive day?

I had won the race and received two nights in a 5-star hotel and Megan had won her age category for women and so won a single night in a 4-star. That left us short by one night but Paul was under 20 years old and he won the Junior race and so we had our four nights!

After the prize giving we all collected our bags and split up to relax and sleep in luxury for one night in one of the four or five star hotels. It was a nice change from our regular hostel style and we still laugh about those times.

Singapore Spin

Frank Tooley

Visiting this Island City for the first time to attend the Formula 1 Grand Prix, I take advantage of my jet lag to get up well before dawn to run before the ill effects of the temperature and humidity. No weather forecast necessary here; 31 degrees every day as it's virtually on the Equator. I get some very odd looks from the staff as I exit the hotel, since street running is simply not done here and I see no other runners pounding the pavements all week. It is a short run down Stamford Rd. (named after Raffles Stamford on whose efforts the city rose to prominence) and then up Government Hill to Fort Canning Park. This is of great interest to me as it was my father's place of work in the 50s. He was stationed here as a Warrant Officer in the British Army. The contrast between how my sister and parents experienced the city then and how it looks now is surely the most extreme of any city. I make my way past the park's many 'specimen' trees to the lighthouse, bizarrely situated in the centre of the city. This was once the highest point of Singapore but is now surrounded and dwarfed by the city's modern architecture, and further inland after extensive land reclamation.

Around the park and out across the Singapore River, I'm in Clark Quay which is strangely deserted; last night it was gridlock here, standing room only in every bar, and every restaurant at capacity. I run downstream to one of the few buildings to have remained unchanged since my family lived here; the 5 star Fullerton Hotel which was formerly the General Post Office building. I next loop around the Marina which is full of impressive yachts reminiscent of other Marina Grand Prix: Monaco, Abu Dhabi and Valencia. I eventually reach the engineering wonder that currently dominates the Singapore skyline – the 200 meter tall Marina Bay Sands Hotel. The gravity-defying Sands SkyPark is set on top of three lambda-shaped towers. Like a cantilevered horizontal Eiffel tower in length, it appears to be a super-tanker parked on top of the buildings. Many workers are now starting to arrive to start their working day on the massive buildings going up around it, and I'm once again greeted by more puzzled looks as running is clearly not a normal hobby here. I take the East Coast Parkway across the Singapore River again towards the Singapore Flyer which at 165 m is the world's tallest observation wheel (London Eye is 'only' 135 m). The previous day we stayed on it for two revolutions, refusing to exit after one turn as a huge lightning storm was about to hit the city and we wanted to watch it from this vantage point.

The Flyer is close to the grandstand area of the track and I am frustrated in finding my way back to the Hotel by the closure of many roads for the race. Eventually I run back along St Andrew's Road past the Padong Cricket Ground where my father played first class cricket and where tonight, after the race, we will watch Mariah Carey in concert.

Yes, it's Singapore, but not as my family would recognise it!

Asking Directions

David Syme

It is dangerous to try to squeeze in a quick run in unknown territory, as I found out in Krakow in September 2010. The weather had been wet and windy for most of our short city break, but on Sunday, the final day, the sun broke through in the afternoon. I made some calculations in my head as we returned from the salt mines at Wieliczka with a few hours of unprogrammed leisure before the evening concert. As our coach deposited us at the Novotel I said to my wife that I would just be able to squeeze in a quick run. The plan approved, I changed quickly into my running kit. The walk round the Old Town (Stare Miasto) on the first day had sown the seed. Our guide pointed to a section of crumbling masonry and told us that this was all that remained of the old city wall. Replacing the wall was a ring of grass with paths, trees and flower beds, she said. I am sure that I am not the first to see this as good run potential! The Old Town is not very big, so I confidently added some distance by crossing the River Vistula to enjoy good views of Wawel Castle from the far bank. It was good to stretch the legs, and I noticed that many others were taking advantage of the sunshine to enjoy a good walk. Once back on the city side of the river I skirted the castle hill to pick up the green ring which was to take me anticlockwise round the Old Town until I could see the blue neon NOVOTEL sign and head for home.

The gardens were very popular! I tried to keep to the perimeter path, but had to weave in and out, avoiding pram-pushers, dog walkers, skate boarders and courting couples. Cyclists had all this – and me – to contend with! It was busy, but enjoyable. At the furthest point from our hotel the perimeter path was fenced off for repair work. I could keep right by taking a subway under the Basztowa Ring Road rather than go back a few metres and take a route off to the left. There was time to add on a few minutes by doing this, so I took the subway and emerged on the far side of the road into a pleasant, wide square. I decided to explore the square, and enjoyed a good look around, then continued in what I thought was roughly the right direction to find a street parallel to Baszowta. I would soon take a left, cross the busy ring road and continue through the park. I must have misjudged the angles somewhat.... I ran alongside the railway station, then railway track, aware that a left turn would be a good idea, but there was none for quite some distance! This 'squeezed-in' run was not meant to be a city tour, so I upped the tempo and charged through sleepy residential streets with little to help me navigate back to the centre.

My Polish is limited, but I was preparing to ask directions using single words and signs when I next saw someone. As I passed a doorway I saw a young chap standing on the step, smoking. What made me screech to a halt was the fact that he was wearing a black jacket, kilt and white stockings! I asked him in English which way to the Old Town. He looked at me in surprise for a moment, then threw his head back and shouted "Jamie!" A first floor window opened and Jamie's head emerged, cigarette between the lips, his hands still wrestling with a bow tie. "Which way tae the auld toon?"

"Left!" And Jamie's head disappeared. The young lad explained that Jamie was to be married in 20 minutes to a Krakow girl he had met in Livingston. My time was drawing to a close, so I shot off left, found the park and slalomed through other park-users back to the hotel, just in time to shower, change and meet the tour group in the foyer at the appointed time. The extra distance and time pressure had added urgency to my run, so I had had a good workout and seen Krakow people relaxing on a Sunday afternoon in their beautiful Old Town. All in all, a great run, worth squeezing in.

Good luck to Jamie and his Polish bride!

Consolation Run

David Syme

Pat and I decided to take a fly/drive holiday in South Africa, starting in the south and going up to the Drakensberg Mountains. I looked up the website of the Cathedral Peak Hotel. "Every day there is a programme of walks which will be conducted by local guides. Write your name on the sheet and meet by the fountain if you wish to take part. On Wednesday there will be a guided excursion to Cathedral Peak for those in good condition. This walk is long and strenuous, and will start at 7 am and take 10–12 hours. Ask for a packed lunch if you plan to go."

Sitting at home in Scotland and reading the hotel web page I had been drawn to this excursion. The only physical challenges on our Jan/Feb fly-drive tour of South Africa would be snatched early morning runs, so I looked forward to a full day of hard walking. Although packing to meet the airline weight limit had been out of my hands, I managed to include several items which would be useful on a hill day. I couldn't wait…

The webpage had failed to tell us just how rainy the rainy season could be! It poured. The hotel had an inadequate supply of golf brollies, and I had to identify a departing guest and buy him a drink before I could get my hands on one. We managed some of the shorter walks, but ended them soaked to the skin. Our bedroom was a drying area; we used anything that we could – lamps, picture rails, pelmets – to hang out damp garments. On Tuesday evening the Deputy General Manager, Erroll, approached me. Mine was the only name on the list for Wednesday's walk to Cathedral Peak. The thing is, he said, the rivers on the way up are impassable, so a huge detour will be necessary. Then the slabs near the summit will be very, very slippery, leeches will be active, and the forecast is for more rain overnight. As a dissuading speech it was fairly blunt, but I did not want to make an issue. I asked if there was another long but safer challenge. He offered me the Ribbon Falls – Tarn Hill – Mushroom Rock circular walk. He described it as a strenuous walk of 5 hours, and I decided to run it.

I took an early breakfast of more than my fair share of juice and two bananas, and left the dining room just after 8.30 am. The road went uphill from the car park so I settled into an easy rhythm. This was going to be a long run with some climbing, and there was no point in rushing, was there? Soon I left the road and turned left. The rain had almost stopped, leaving a greasy surface to the muddy red path. The tall wet grasses on either side brushed against my legs, white crabs scuttled across the path, and a heron flapped its way down the valley. Small prints and a freshly-dropped porcupine quill showed that mine were not the first feet on the path that morning.

To my left was the lush valley I would drop into. I could only see the lower slopes as thick mist lay over the upper area. A Y-shape of white water clearly showed the small river I would have to cross at its junction. The right-hand stream came down from Doreen Falls, which was the turning point of one of the shorter walks, but my route led up through the mist onto the shoulder which came down between the two streams. At the crossing point the stepping stones were a good foot under fast-moving water, so I explored the right-hand branch. Before long I discovered a place narrow enough for me to jump over. First I decided to go up to the waterfall, and found it to be impressive; the water shooting over a flat lip and, 20m below, forming a wide, seething, swirling pool of dark brown. I was glad I'd made the detour.

Safely over the stream I started up the shoulder. It steepened dramatically, so running became impossible and I settled for a determined walk. Where the ridge became a rock face the path contoured round until it found a weakness and a scramble brought me to top of that rock. I soon entered the mist and worked my way upwards, concentrating on foot placement. I'm not sure if the baboon saw me before I saw it, but we were both pretty startled! It was only a few feet away as my head came silently up and over a large rock, but it was 50 yards away by the time my feet reached that level! After the steep section I was almost up to the escarpment when the mist started to clear away. In the deep valley on my right I could just make out another attraction – Ribbon Falls. Normally a fine white vertical line of falling water, today it was gushing dark-red and angry, with a cloud of spray rising from the pool below.

This part of the escarpment is featureless rolling grassland apart from two distinct humps (called The Camel) . Erroll had told me that the path was indistinct, but to aim west for the humps until I reached an old jeep track. As the grass is long I almost jogged onto the track before I saw it, but turned confidently to the right and relaxed into a pleasant trot, being for the first time on level ground. I saw partridge, buck and eland, and even three black-backed jackals but was surprised that such a broad expanse of lush grass offered so few grazing animals. The track was too good to last, and before long I could see only traces of it. When I had lost anything resembling a track or path I continued north until I found myself approaching another hump. It seemed a good idea to go to the top for a 360 degree orientation, so I did. I checked out a dip to the south of the summit and found a reedy pond. This had to be Tarn Hill! From here, Erroll had told me, I should keep to the eastern rim of the escarpment, so I consulted my compass and was picking my way along the edge when the clouds parted, giving me a fine view of the valley beneath me and the foothills to the north. Where Cathedral Peak lay there were still heavy clouds. The clearing sky meant that I was also able to see ahead my next way-marker, Mushroom Rock, which Pat and I had visited earlier in the week. No more navigational challenges, then! Instead I gave myself another challenge. Could I make it back to the hotel for their 11–1130 am coffee trolley? It was all downhill, very steep in places and slippery underfoot. Reason argued that it was not terrain to hurry on, but reason was no match for the memory of the homemade cakes on the coffee trolley! With the clock in my head ticking loudly I slithered my way back down, reaching the trolley with 5 minutes to spare.

After lunch heavy rain came once more, hissing down onto the walkways and forming brown puddles in the grass. The golf course was closed and hotel guests were wandering through the lobby, queuing for the one internet terminal or snoozing in the lounge. I could face the depressing weather with glowing cheeks and the memory of the morning's solo run. It wasn't the mountain walk I had hoped for, but as a consolation run it ticked several boxes!

New Direction

Roy Cunningham

Roy is a friend of David Syme's and lives in Balerno. He is a company CEO whose sporting passions are mountain-biking, fishing and skiing. He also likes running and recently went on holiday with the family in Les Contamines in the French Alps with a copy of Running Away From Home *in his luggage.*

After another few chapters of THAT book (Mairi and James were amazed to see me for the first time actually reading and laughing out loud) I just had to share the following from earlier today, while I'm waiting for the rain to clear.

Up before the rest of the family (not unusual) I looked at my running shoes resting against the wall outside the patio window. They called to me: "Let's just go for a half hour run round the valley floor…" My usual gentle run leads me up the riverside trail to the Gorge chapel, turn right down the road to Du Lay – back at the apartment in time for breakfast.

So off we went, my running shoes and I, and once I had recovered my altitude breath and settled into a nice pace along the trail a voice started nag-nagging at me. What if I were to go left and not right at the Chapel…? "Go left at the chapel, go left! I'll bet Dave Syme would go left! What new experience lies left? As he says in the book, it could be memorable! I know from the map that there are higher-altitude trails coming back down the valley, I'm sure I can find them. Once higher up I'll know the turn-off for our village from skiing up there. I bet Dave would say left…" And before I knew it I had past the chapel bridge and was heading left and up the Tour de Mont Blanc trail.

I managed to keep myself running, a slow short-paced jog, for the first 5 minutes or so but was soon forced to change to a fast walk, passing the booted and pole-waving trekkers making the start to their day up on the high tops. Soon the incline relented slightly, and, buoyed on by the motivation of jogging past the ambling walkers who were all startled as I puffed past, I made good progress to the Pont Romain waterfall, which we had passed last summer when descending onto this route from the Roselette ski area. Here I remembered seeing a path to the left which I was sure would take me back down the valley along the high terraces and balconies of Le Bon Nant river.

To begin with I continued to climb, this time with a spring in my step and a smile at being in new territory. I had really found my breath now and was enjoying the changing terrain which was passing under me at a decent rate. I reached a sign saying 1580m and started along the level path which flowed between trees and rock walls, occasionally catching glimpses of the river and mountain slopes opposite through the dense pine forest.

Then a surprise. The trail dropped into another small valley not visible from our own and I wound my way up another climb over small cascading streams which flowed across my trail, up into the main Les Contamines valley once more.

I was now very aware that my 30 min run had lasted 50 mins and I was over 500m above the village, somewhere down below and I still didn't know where I was going to come out. I passed several trails going right and up, so I kept going looking for the one to the left and down to where I suspected trouble would be brewing about my absence.

Then there it was… a trail on the left. Definitely going down. Steeply! After a couple of careful slips and slides on the loose gravel I loped down a wonderful series of switch-backs cut into the hill to ease the ascent of the walkers making for some high summit.

The trees cleared and I was granted the most fantastic view

of Les Contamines with Saint Gervais in the distance, the ski slopes of Etape across the valley and the leisure park with its early morning swimmers and tennis players below me.... I almost stopped to drink it in but with my balance well set I continued my run downwards and into the trees below once more. Here I found a fire road which cut its way right this time, with a gentle down-slope which allowed me to open up. Soon I started to hear the familiar clatter from the biathlon shooting range, and knew I was close to the road and half a mile from the apartment.

Arriving at the terrace fence 'la famille' was gathered round the table at breakfast and I was greeted with a "You're mad! Where have you been?" Ah, but that baguette and myrtle jam tasted so good... thank you, Mr Syme!

Greek and Roman Odysseys

Frank Tooley

In Athens to present at a workshop on company start-ups, I took advantage of the hotel's central location to 'do Athens' before the meeting began at 9 am. I was out well before dawn and the dreadful traffic that blights the city and ran to the Lykavittos Hill, the top of which is the highest point in Athens. It's an easy 910 ft climb through a park with mature olive trees and the panorama of the coast and mountains in the distance; the city laid out below was particularly breathtaking as dawn broke. The Parthenon on the Acropolis Hill looked magnificent with the early sun casting deep colourful shadows. I was the only person there excepting two smartly-uniformed soldiers who, with great ceremony despite no-one watching them, ran up the Greek flag on the flagpole outside the whitewashed St George's Chapel. Taking careful bearings, I set off for the Acropolis Hill. A few miles later, I was at the locked gates into the park- disappointed as I had hoped to run up the Hill to see the ruins but the park doesn't open until 10 am. I circled the hill and got lost in the maze of streets, churches and ruined temples eventually ending up at the central fish market just as it was closing – a barn of a place that was an assault on the senses. Then back to the Hotel before the conference – 9 glorious miles.

In Rome on holiday, Elaine Scott and I left our spouses still asleep and continued our training for upcoming London and

Edinburgh marathons with a Sunday dawn run. The additional benefit of this is that we did the sights without any jostling crowds and traffic. We jogged the 2 miles past the Forum to the Coliseum and ran around it – it's a magnificent structure with the three tiers comprised of from top to bottom: Corinthian, Ionic and Doric columns. Just around the corner we ran around the Circus Maximus whilst thinking about chariot races (Ben Hur). From there we ran past the La Bocca della Verità (Month of Truth) familiar from Roman Holiday (Peck and Hepburn). Then over the Tiber by bridge; bad form for a Triathlete, I know – I should have swum across but the river was in spate and a rather frightening colour and consistency (old fiats and pizza boxes). Down the Via della Conciliazione to St Peter's Square which was empty apart from a few Swiss Guards in their harlequin suits. Back past the Castel Sant Angelo (you know, the one from Angels and Demons) then over the Tiber again and to the Pantheon (not allowed in as shorts not a suitable attire for a church). Then on to Piazza di Spagna and up the Spanish Steps and eventually getting lost a few times before finding the Trevi Fountain, back to the hotel. About 8 miles but took nearly 2 hours as we kept stopping to take photos.

What better way to explore these ancient and wonderful cities than an early morning run?

I'd Run across Continents for Love

Elizabeth Kamm

Elizabeth wrote these words in November 2009 after she and her boyfriend had broken up. She runs her own business in London; fitness training for post natal and pre natal ladies, as well as busy mums-on-the-run **www.lovefitbetsy.com**

Running through life with a special someone is a wonderful thing. Especially when you have a passion for running, and the person dearest to your heart does too.

Running in Paris, hand in hand around the Arc de Triumph in the rain… getting lost in a Parisian park, finding yourself kissing because you don't know which way to turn, hearing a fountain in the background and feeling the cool droplets of rain dripping over your head whilst feeling the warmth of someone's body as they embrace you with a loving bear hug.

Running in Ipswich, a race for charity. You're running as fast as you can through the forest whilst your loved one is cycling and egging you on, "You've got 'im! Come on, run faster!"

Running in Scotland, the Rob Roy Challenge, in June. For 16 miles cross country, we stormed our way to arrive 6th and 7th on the first leg of the challenge. Sadly, my running legs weren't so strong on a bike, and other teams overtook us. For both it was still a great experience.

Florence in July, my 36th birthday. In the morning we ran south over the river towards a gently sloping hill which took us to a large, open square where our views of Florence were spectacular. The heat of the sun beating down whilst the salty sweat dripped off us. Racing up the steps to the top of the hill... who could get there first? It was a photo finish! The beauty of the place I will never forget.

Istanbul, an interesting place. We ran across continents – from Europe over the Bosphorus to Asia. It made the London air seem fresh. Hot-footing along the banks of the channel, fishing boats bobbing high on the water, fishermen sitting calmly awaiting their prey, with such a blue-skied morning... before the heavens opened and our warm, dry kit became heavy and wet. A Turkish man trying to flog us umbrellas, found it amusing when we ran past gesticulating that they would be hopeless for the drowned rats we already were.

Running in Aberdeenshire! The country smells and the tranquillity of the place, picking our way across the golf course before heading home. A cheeky kiss under the arched bridge of a tiny, sleepy village. We may have been spotted? We may have been the talk of the toon!

Greenwich Park, a regular Monday run for us. Along with Clapham, Wandsworth, Chelsea Embankment and Richmond Park. Great chats and lots of ideas, every time, it didn't matter where we were. We always had a feeling of exhilaration and happiness at the end. Smiling broadly (sometimes grimacing) and thanking each other for inspiring each other, once again.

And now I'm back to the beginning. A half marathon is planned for us in two weeks' time. But my loved one has run away. He's scared. Scared to feel so alive and happy, scared to commit and fail. We have come so far since we ran the Royal Parks Half Marathon a year ago. On that occasion my legs took me on a faster journey and I crossed the finishing line first. This time round my beloved has already reached the finishing line, because he is too scared to keep running.

POSTSCRIPT

Elizabeth and Andrew have since been reunited and are very happy together. They plan to be so for a long time to come.

Farewell to Europe

Ammended extract from *Running Beyond Limits*,
by Andrew Murray

Andrew is a GP, a Sports and Exercise Medicine doctor whose passion is getting and keeping people active. He is also a runner, and the author of the acclaimed Running Beyond Limits, *published by Mountain Media, foreword by Sir Ran Fiennes. He has been running since 2005 when he realized that it might be a good way to see a bit of the world.*

Since then he has won first place in numerous endurance races in some of the strangest venues in the world, including the Arctic, the Sahara and Outer Mongolia. He won the prestigious North Pole Marathon in 2012. Temperatures at these events have ranged from -70 to +45 degrees celsius. On the other hand, Andrew has also been overtaken by a donkey, and a nine-year old boy while running 2659 miles from the far north of Scotland to the Moroccan Sahara – www. scotland2sahara – a run that has raised over £78,000 thus far for www. yamaatrust.com, a charity that tackles poverty in the south Gobi region of Mongolia. That run also inspired over 1200 people to accompany Andrew on part of the route and was the subject of an hour-long BBC documentary.

As an expedition/event doctor Andrew has worked on six continents and the geographic North Pole where he has been able to study the effects of extreme conditions on some of the toughest athletes in the world.

The dramatic escarpments of Ronda lay behind us. This birthplace of modern bull fighting, with its fairy tale style bridge, had inspired Orson Welles and Ernest Hemmingway and it had been good enough for the Murrays. Birds had sung, and the sun shone, as we gazed down on the escarpments that had repelled the Crusaders.

The natural aesthetics of the surrounding area dulled any pain in my Achilles tendons, which resembled two sticks of rhubarb. The views were much more effective than paracetamol. Passing Ernest Hemmingway's former house, I had stood and chatted to Dad on the bridge, peering 120 metres down into the canyon below. It was Mum's birthday, a date she shares with Elvis Presley, and Ronda seemed an appropriate place for celebration as we ate a picnic lunch just outside the town. Perhaps I had over-indulged, as my food reappeared as soon as I hit the uphill, causing two members of the friendly local constabulary to pull over and ask me to vomit further from the road if I would be so kind. This pair, one of which was a double for Mahoney from Police Academy, kept a close eye on me for several hundred metres as I sloped off skyward at a snail's pace towards the high pass on the Algeciras road. The switchbacks that descended from the pass were magnificent, with distant peaks sparkling in the distance. It was impossible not to grin widely.

Mum's birthday supper was pizza, and we ate it while watching a thunderstorm roll in at Benadalid. Rain thrashed around us, causing a brief powercut, as I considered my course of action. Tomorrow would be amazing. Almost certainly we'd see Africa, and, as we were at 800 metres of altitude, there would have to be ample downhill. It was over 45 miles to the port of Algeciras, but the lure of Africa was strong. It felt like Christmas Eve.

The following day I saw an 'Algeciras 80km' sign. Was it worth doing the distance and making the crossing that night? Dad, sporting his Active Nation Scotland shirt came running with me. My parents had taken me to live in Africa at the age of two, and brought me up while working in a mission hospital in Kenya for six years. I couldn't have asked for a happier childhood. I was truly privileged to grow up in this way, and was proud that two of my greatest role models and inspirations would join me as Africa drew us towards her. Dense scrub morphed into orange groves as the

Straits of Gibraltar approached. The heat cranked up at the lower altitude. I got speaking to Chris, a triathlete from Gibraltar who was up training in the mountains. He explained the history of the Rock and its inhabitants and it sounded splendid, but another local countered, "it's terrible, like Britain but with monkeys." I thought that sounded pretty good too. Everything happens more slowly at the speed of a runner. Chris sped off while cars thundered past. The clouds gathered menacingly overhead, whilst chickens scurried around an orange grove.

My mind wandered. I'd been reading *Born to Run* by Christopher McDougall. I read a theory stating that Homo Sapiens had prevailed, while the Neanderthals had become extinct in part due to our superior ability to run for hours on end, enduring the heat and other inconveniences whilst pursuing prey relentlessly. Despite the greater strength and larger brains of the Neanderthals, they had lacked this ability. An African sky opened before us. For all the time I'd spent running solo, and all the time this offered to reflect, I'd enjoyed my run with Dad. The loneliness of the long distance runner becomes boring at times. With his company had come a bond, a shared understanding of the pleasures and difficulties and the chance to laugh and unwind. I knew he'd been supporting me throughout my entire run from John O' Groats to the Sahara, but on this leg our physical proximity brought this home. We remembered Kenya, and the natural athletic ability of the children there. Most of the world's top distance runners come from East Africa, many from the Kalenjin tribe, which make up about 12% of Kenya's population. Kalenjin athletes have won about 40% of international medals available in long distance running since 1980 which is a mind blowing statistic for a tribe that represents less than 0.001% of the world's population. I hadn't inherited any of their brilliance at long distance running, but shared the enthusiasm for it.

I jogged into the port, arriving as the sun set on Europe. The downhill and the company had made the 80kms a pleasure. Across the water Morocco's Rif Mountains rose inexorably from the sea. I'd completed my European leg, running 261 miles that week and 2130 miles in total. I had now run across four countries, with only Morocco to go. This for me is what running is all about: freedom and exploration. My route showed me running through ancient cities, the mighty Atlas Mountains, verdant gorges before finally traversing the high sand dunes on the Algerian border. I'd be taking two weeks to run what I'd previously covered in three days in a jeep. I took leave of my parents and boarded the ferry, then hunted down a raft of pasta meals and wolfed them down voraciously. It would be the Moroccan staples of cous cous and stew all the way to the finish from here.

The ship's horn sounded as we inched away from the quay. A new continent awaited.

Andrew with his parents in Spain

The Rotten Apple

Andrew Syme

Runs away from home are highlights in a running year. New routes, sights, smells, or temperatures with the exciting slight worry of getting lost make them something special – most of the time. Occasionally, as in a basket of delicious fresh apples, there can be the rotten one. I had my 'rotten apple' on the island of Fuerteventura and I'd like to share some of my pain and discomfort with you.

As usual on holiday I like to run before breakfast; best temperatures, quiet paths and not claiming precious time on a family holiday. This time I left the hotel room at 6.40 am and felt the back of my heel rubbing as I walked to the lift. Yesterday's run had subtly angered the heel area and now with the wrong socks I was destined for a run of pain. A sensible person would have then cancelled the run, I could have gone to the cycle machine in the fitness room but I somehow convinced myself: it won't hurt when I'm running!

I started jogging from the hotel down the coast on a firm sandy path between the sea and the main road. The heel was rubbing badly and already bleeding after 5 minutes so I stopped and tied the laces so tightly there was no more loose rubbing, but blood circulation to the toes was completely cut off.

I remember thinking, trying to get in a positive frame of mind, that after a week and 7 runs I still had not had an unplanned toilet stop, when, at that moment, my stomach started to boil and churn. I found a secluded spot behind a dyke and relieved myself, thankful of the toilet paper I always have with me. Not wanting to leave the eyesore of white toilet paper I had the brilliant idea of throwing a flat stone over my deeds which, without going into detail, had about the same effect as stamping on a water balloon. I hobbled on; my left heel was not rubbing but the bridge of the foot was hurting due to the tight laces. The sun was rising over the Atlantic and I was on a lovely path – it should be a great run, I kept trying to convince myself.

After unusually heavy rain in the previous two days the path was still muddy – mud the likes of which I have never seen before. There was no telling what was firm ground and what was mud so I ran straight into the first mud 'trap'. This mix of clay and mud was so sticky that within two steps both shoes were covered in a thick layer of this pale brown substance, two steps later I was in sand, so the result was a weight on the feet as if I were wearing ski boots! Of course with this weight the rubbing started again on the heel now with the added highlight of sand and mud getting into the open wound. I checked my GPS watch. I'd planned to run 11km, turning at 5.5km but saw that after my toilet stop I'd forgotten to re-press the start button so the km count was stuck at 2.13. I trudged on.

Of course a bad run has to have its dog incident! This was a ferocious black beast that jumped towards me in its garden, barking like crazy and obviously keen on having me for breakfast. The fence was just high enough to stop it coming over but with one mighty leap it might just... I sped up ignoring the increased heel pain.

The path went down a hill to sea level in a small bay area then up the other side. At the path's lowest point I had to cross a small burn, just avoiding getting my feet wet by leaping from stone to stone. I jogged up the other side, a bit further then turned around after approximately 1km and thankfully headed back. Just before re-crossing the burn I hit another bit of mud and decided while I was at the sea to relieve my shoes of this extra weight. I carefully cleaned the sides and soles of my shoes of this chewing gum-like substance, making sure my shoes stayed as dry as possible. Time to cross the burn – but where were my stones! – in the 15 minutes since I'd crossed over the tide had come in so much that the stones were completely submerged. I had to wade across mid-shin deep with whoops of agony as the salt attacked the open wounds, now on both heels.

I plodded home in misery, close to tears and wondering why on earth I was doing this when I should be still in bed. After what felt like a marathon I reached the hotel and limped with squelching shoes to my room, the next diarrhoea pains already causing my stomach to make sounds like a boiling kettle.

As I entered the room feeling like a wounded but triumphant gladiator, my wife asked how was my run, I replied, "It was okay, thanks" as I thought about my running route for the next morning…

'Zeit ist egal'

Ann Davidson

I'd always wanted to visit Berlin but it was my decision to run the marathon that finally got me there. We had left it quite late to book a hotel so we ended up renting an apartment instead. It was a superb place, spacious and well-equipped but not quite as close to the marathon start as it looked on the map. (Berlin is a much bigger city than either of us had realised.)

In the days leading up to a marathon I like to do a fair bit of walking but very little running. That was fine – it gave us the chance to do plenty of sightseeing. The race Expo had been moved to a new venue and we gave ourselves plenty of time to get there, arriving before it opened. Just as well! By the time we came out of the Expo having collected my race pack, been to the pasta party and visited the exhibition halls (one is for roller-blade marathon participants) the roads outside were gridlocked and the queues enormous.

On the day before the race we walked from our apartment to the start/finish area. As we passed the zoo we saw lots of people standing outside the entrance. They were laying flowers and paying tribute to a zookeeper who had died suddenly. He had become famous by refusing to allow the zoo authority to have a polar bear cub put down because it was surplus to requirements. The bear, named Knut, was identified with the bear which is the symbol of Berlin and the keeper became a local hero.

We got to the marathon area where everything was already set up. Suddenly, it all seemed very real. We watched the start of the roller-blade marathon which is a truly amazing sight. 20,000 roller skaters setting off in waves, many of them in speed skating teams. Each member would take a turn to lead then slip back to the end of the team line. It was a really impressive sight. Following them were people who just wanted to complete the marathon on skates, some clearly more able than others, with marshals quick to help anyone who fell. It really was an all-ability event.

On race day things didn't go quite as planned. We had somehow miscalculated how long it would take to walk to the start and I was almost running as we arrived. Thousands of runners were already lined up in the start pens and I still had to drop my bag off. Fortunately, one of the stewards took pity on us and agreed that my husband (a non-runner) could drop my bag off for me at the baggage tent.

There was a huge cheer for Haile Gebresellassie as he took his place at the head of the elite field to defend his world record. Much, much further back I stood waiting to take part in the race. As the elite runners headed off and we walked up towards the start line I overheard two runners discussing their hoped for results when a voice beside me said, "Zeit ist egal." (time doesn't matter). I just wanted to finish upright and smiling, so I had to agree.

The hooter sounded for us, the last group to start and we set off along the beautiful tree lined streets. The skies overhead were clear and blue, no sign of the clouds that had been promised in weather forecasts in the past few days.

The course was packed with people, some of them walking, so it was quite hard work just finding a way past people. The first sign I saw was 4km – I couldn't believe we'd come so far already. By 5km people were starting to complain about the heat. It was really warm now and the first water station was a welcome sight. Water was handed out in plastic cups so you had to stop and drink or you ended up with it slopped all over you! Apparently this is to reduce the environmental impact of the race, but it would be nice to get a bottle you could hang on to and run with.

At 7km I heard my husband shouting from the crowd – that put a big smile on my face as I didn't expect him to be there. 10km in and I felt really good, just a bit hot. All along the route people were clapping, whistling and making a noise. There were lots of bands too and that really helped keep everyone feeling positive.

I checked my watch as I reached the half marathon stage – 2.07. That meant Haile Gebreselassie was already finished and I still had a half marathon to run!

The entire population of Denmark seemed to be taking part with red t-shirts everywhere and lots of shouts of "Denmark" from the crowd. I even passed a lady running in traditional Danish costume. As we reached the next water station I saw a poor man in a polar bear outfit – and I thought I was feeling the heat! Some of the stations were handing out tea (honestly!) and a sports drink called Basica (not as sweet as Lucozade Sport or Gatorade). This was in paper cups so again you had to stop to drink. The road was really sticky after every refreshment stop where the drinks had been spilled and dropped.

26km and by now I only had 10 miles to go (I can still work out that 10 miles is 16km at this stage – not bad!) I felt very hot and a bit sunburned but the legs were OK and fortunately many of the streets were tree-lined and offered some very welcome shade. By now I needed something to eat but I couldn't manage my cereal bar until I got more water. Thankfully the stations were every few kilometres so I didn't have to wait too long. I avoided the 'showers' created by fire engine hoses though – they were a bit too cold for me!

I reached the 32km feeling surprisingly good but I knew the

final 10km would be the toughest. However, it was only as I got to the last 5km that my legs started to feel heavy, my feet were burning and I was just fed up of weaving past walking people. We turned into a quiet side street – the only place on the course where there were no supporters – and it felt like I still had ages to go. But just as quickly we turned the corner and I was running up Unter den Linden, the wide avenue that leads to the Brandenburg Gate. The noise was deafening and I could even forgive the spectators shouting, "Hop! Hop! Hop!" (It's hard enough running at this stage – trust me, hopping is not on the agenda!) I could see the edge of the Gate now and I knew I didn't have far to go. The race doesn't end at the Gate, but continues for another 400m with grandstands on either side.

As I ran through the Brandenburg Gate (what a feeling!) I focused on my plan for the finish. Halfway between the gate and the line is a statue on the left. When I reached that I was going to give everything I'd got for a big finish. And then suddenly something incredible happened. I heard the sound of bagpipes playing, and the crowd was clapping and cheering, and I was clapping and cheering too, and on the big screen I could see a kilted piper striding to the line and I just wanted to catch him and thank him. I just felt so thrilled as I neared the finish and the announcer shouted, "Well done, Scotland!" and I was really proud of the little saltire on the back of my running vest. I reached the mat, stopped my watch and thanked the piper, who was delighted to meet a fellow Scot. (His name was Scott Crighton and he had arranged to have his kilt and pipes waiting for him at the Gate so he could finish in style. I was just lucky to arrive when I did.)

I'd completed the course in 4.19 – not my fastest marathon, but definitely my best. I'm sure Haile Gebreselassie was delighted when he crossed the line in 2.03.59 but I was just as pleased with how things turned out for me – Zeit ist egal!

New York, New York!

David Syme

As the years pass, memories of races become blurred and only the highlights remain clear in the mind. For one race, maybe a successful bid for a PB, in another a particular hill (who can forget the one in Phoenix Park near the end of Dublin Marathon!) or a friendship struck up with a fellow competitor. For me the most vivid memory of the New York City Marathon on 4th November 2001 will always be the start.

My son Andrew, daughter Fiona and I submitted our entries for the New York City Marathon in the summer of 2001 through a charity called 'Get Kids Going', and set about squeezing sponsorship money from friends and family. Training was an individual matter – one of us being in London, one in Germany and one in Scotland, but we supported each other by comparing training times and distances. And then the 9/11 terrorists struck...

After the shock, horror and confusion of the 9th September, calm slowly returned. Comparatively few runners backed out of the race. We and others held the view that any cancellation represented a victory for terrorism, and carried on training. Nevertheless our meeting at Heathrow on 01 November was emotionally charged, being a family reunion, preparing for a flight shortly after the attacks and the first stage to a famous marathon.

Entry to USA at Newark was not pleasant, as the Immigration

staff worked slowly and cautiously, armed police lurking nearby. The cold atmosphere of the airport Immigration Hall was soon forgotten as numerous New Yorkers thanked us for coming to their city at this time. Our accommodation in the Vanderbildt YMCA had been chosen for its room rate and its proximity to the Finish in Central Park, not for its comfort. It offered the cheerful chaos you always find in hotels before a big race. On the day before the race we had a busy day of sight-seeing which included a visit to pay our respects at Ground Zero (still smoking) from a viewing platform, and the Empire State Building, from the top of which we could compare the actual skyline with the pre-September panorama board… a chilling moment.

There had been some worrying threats of terrorist disruption of the race, and runners were urged to reach the start area very early so that bridges could be closed and checked for explosives. As a result they organised shuttle buses to start taking runners from Grand Central Station to the Start from 5 am, and we were in one of the first buses. It was still dark, but the sky was clear and it was wind-free and cool.

The Start area was huge and very well-organised. It boasts the world's longest men's urinal, and the ladies were equally well treated in that respect. So, there we were, three and a half hours till kick-off and nothing to do. We sat, watched the world go by and the sun come up, listened to live jazz music and we talked. We discussed possibilities for our next race, how we would run this one, where we might meet afterwards and what we fancied to eat that evening… With half an hour to go it was time to wish each other good luck and separate to our designated pens. Andrew was aiming for 3 hours, Fiona 4, and I was further back. The public address system was excellent, so everyone who was there will remember the speech by Mayor Rudy Giuliani. He thanked visitors for coming and praised Americans and especially the citizens of his city for their resilience. He acknowledged the city's debt to the Fire Service and the Police, and we had a minute's silence to remember all – but particularly their – victims in the 9/11 attack. Then two singers picked up the microphone, one after the other, just before the start. First came 'The Star-spangled Banner' from a member of Fire Department New York, then we heard a rich tenor voice from New York Police Department who sang 'New York, New York'. Every runner was deeply moved; some hugged each other, some stood with hand over heart, all in a common bond of emotional overload. By the time we pressed forward to start the race there was not a dry eye to be seen. The normal euphoria of a marathon start after a long wait was totally absent; a silent snake of runners pattered over the Verrazano Narrows Bridge and most of us were well into Brooklyn before the normal atmosphere of marathon bonhomie resumed. At my level there were many runners who wore vests with pictures of loved ones lost in the attack; they received sympathetic pats on the back or words of commiseration from others. Every fire station and police precinct was applauded as we passed, and several had pictures of their victims on the walls.

Support was good until we crossed the Queensboro Bridge into Manhattan, then it became tremendous! At the 16 mile point, when you turn right and slightly downhill into 1st Avenue the crowds were in full song, and they needed to be. The lower order runners like me had in front of them a frighteningly long river of bobbing heads. Vocal support was much appreciated! The Finish in Central Park was well-handled, medals were given out, but I could not raise my spirits with the usual "I've done it!" feeling. As well as physically exhausted I felt emotionally drained, and remember walking back to the YMCA in a stupor. It had been a very intense experience.

Yes, the New York City Marathon is one of the biggest running events I have tackled, and it is the only one where the start is the most vivid memory. I have not returned to New York since; until I do it will always be 2001 there for me, and I still feel a shiver run down my spine if I hear on the radio that band play those opening bars: Da da dadada, da da dadada of that song!

A Different Paris

Alexis Badger

I am 31 years old and have been running for about 5 years. Actually, David's daughter, Fiona was one of the people who inspired me to start running more seriously. I became tube-phobic around 5 years ago and I took up running as an alternative way of commuting. I am back on the tube now but running is a habit which I have continued. My other interests are food, long distance walking, travel, fashion and culture. A couple of years ago I walked and cycled 900 km across Spain and I am hoping to do something similar next time I have enough time and money on my hands. I am running the London Marathon in 2012, which I am very much looking forward to.

As I boarded the 06:53 Eurostar to Paris I felt none of the delicious anticipation of previous trips to the city. This time it wasn't about schlepping between gastronomic occasions and high culture; it was about testing my body's limits, enduring pain; I was headed for my first marathon.

Knee and ankle injuries had limited my preparation to one short run and one long run per week. Soft winter days exploring the peaty trails of the High Peak; lonely rain-sodden efforts along the River Mersey; dark nights weaving through groups of exiled smokers on south Manchester's pavements; what if it wasn't enough?

Plummeting self confidence is a hazard of the obligatory trip to the registration centre the day before the event. Packs of lycra'd men and women, all sinewy and lithe of limb, discussed splits and PBs. My self-belief shriveled as I caught sight of my travel-lagged appearance reflected in a window.

I woke up on race day in a tumult of nervous excitement, and

I was relieved to see ordinary people like me among the thousands of runners milling about the start on the Champs Elysees. I started to feel good – if they could do it, I could do it. I was harbouring an ambition to hit 3hrs 30 after surprising myself with some fast training runs, and I couldn't wait to get going.

In the holding pen, frustrated by the queue for the portaloo and panicked by the two minutes to go signal, I followed others' lead and took leave of my dignity, using the slim modesty afforded by a black bin liner to squat and pee in the holding pen. Then we were moving, trudging forward to mile zero through a miasma of urine and discarded plastic bottles.

Adrenaline flooded my body as I crossed the start line and saw the way open up toward the Place de la Concorde. I was flying, and had to focus hard on reining myself in, knowing I couldn't maintain the pace.

The fresh, blue sky morning made the treat of a traffic-free tour of Paris all the more special, and the famed disinterest of the city's residents was not in evidence in the warmth of the crowds. At 8 miles the dappled oak canopy of the Bois de Vincennes provided relief from the sun, and at 14 the majesty of the Cathédrale de Notre Dame distracted from the nagging fear of failure. Then the Eiffel Tower came into view, revealing itself in different aspects as drummers propelled us along the riverside promenade.

Along the Seine the route became a roller coaster of shallow gradients and tungsten-lit tunnels. By 17 miles I started letting others do the hollering on entering the echoing spaces, when Paris disappeared from view and monstrous industrial fans suspended from the roof re-circulated the rarefied air.

I began taking anxious glances at my watch. I had cruised past the half marathon mark in 1:46, knowing that I could have gone faster; now I was struggling to do 9 minute miles. Seeing my discomfort a fellow runner told me I had been pacing him since mile 5 and I couldn't slow down now. It was a nice thing to say, but I could barely muster the energy to acknowledge it.

The crowds began to dissipate at mile 20 as we entered a neighbourhood of forbidding iron gates, protecting the residences of the world's diplomatic corps. No music there, just the sound of feet hitting tarmac and laboured breathing. I focused on propelling myself from my abdomen, barely lifting my legs in an effort to achieve the most efficient stride.

I passed the 22 mile marker, every step now taking me farther than I'd ever run before. I tried to envisage a 4 mile run – not far, but still at least 30 minutes more running on legs so engorged with lactic acid I had the sensation they'd turned to glass, and might shatter with every stride.

Crossing the Bois de Boulogne, so evocative of sedate picnics on a Monet canvas, I wondered if there could be anything more incongruous than thousands of spent marathoners wearing the lawn down to mulch. Picnicking definitely seemed more sensible than what I was doing.

As I turned on to the closing strait, the Avenue Foch, something less polite than foch is what I was thinking as I dug deep and willed the finish line into sight. It helped that the crowd had returned, and the music. I told myself that if I could just get to the end of this in a halfway decent time I would never have to do it again, ever.

Looking like a deranged elephant I produced something approximating a sprint when the end came into view – the concept of my body meeting that line clearing my brain of all other rational thought.

When I crossed it, in 03:38:12, I found myself in the arms of a rather startled German finisher. The salt crust on my face cracked as my facial muscles contracted, producing tears of relief and pride.

I extricated myself from the German, whose initial shock had turned into something more enthusiastic, and tipped a bottle of water over my head, enjoying the sensation of cool liquid trickling down my neck. As I shuffled along to collect my medal I took some of the crowd's cheers all for myself: I had found reserves of discipline and determination I didn't know I had; I'd achieved something I wasn't sure I could do. I had made it. From that day on Paris will always be a special place for me.

Socks Matter

David Syme

My sock drawer is a pit of confusion. When there are three other family runners in the house, laundry distribution is often based on guesswork, especially in the matter of running socks. I will pull out a pair of socks I have never seen before, and I have often noticed my son starting out on a run with a pair of my socks on, and my fear is that these socks will find their way into his suitcase when he prepares to return to his home in Germany. With this in mind I put down a specific request on my Christmas wish list a couple of years ago. I wanted a pair of lime-green running socks.

As other family members were working over Christmas, my wife and I spent the holiday with her San Francisco-based sister, Margaret in Palm Springs. We agreed to take with us any small, light present which we could exchange on Christmas Day, so early on 26th December I set out for a run wearing a new pair of very bright lime-green running socks. Palm Springs is mainly flat, with any undulations made into golf courses. Our hotel was on the western edge, however, and behind us stood a knobbly, treeless, grass-less mountain, an outcrop of the San Jacinto Range. The slopes were of red rock and as I approached and looked closely at it I could not make out any paths. At the peak, however, I saw a small structure which looked like a view indicator, so thought that there had to be a path climbing up to it from somewhere. I ran to the hill and followed the road round its base. After 15 minutes I came to a car-park far from any buildings. At the mountain end of it I noticed a signpost for paths. This was what I wanted! The uphill sign pointed to my viewpoint, and up I ran. The path was well made; it had a firm surface and tackled the hill at a sensible angle, so that I could keep up a good rhythm. After 45 minutes or so I approached the top and was rewarded with a spectacular view in bright early morning sunshine. To the west lay ridge after ridge of rugged, red mountains, to the east Palm Springs lay at my feet with its neat crisscross street pattern punctuated by these golf courses, and to the north I could make out the yellow sandy hills of Joshua Tree Park. The context of this moment was that we had endured an earthquake 4 days earlier, which had been followed by 48 hours of torrential rain and bitter cold. I stood at the viewpoint and admired the scene until the cold air persuaded me to head for home. Still intoxicated by the beauty of the scene I picked my way down the first part of the slope. Can anything top that? I asked. Well… at that point I spotted someone running up the path towards me. I soon made out that the runner was fast and female. Her head was down as she concentrated on her foot placement, so I could watch her progress without my observation causing embarrassment. She was a bonny lass, with short, blonde hair, a white T-shirt and despite the cold a skimpy pair of red shorts above long, shapely brown legs. Perhaps earlier than necessary I stood aside to allow this vision of loveliness to float past me. She glanced up and saw me when we were merely 5 metres apart. She looked me up and down and smiled a delightful smile, then she said two words to me which I'll never forget.

"Neat sacks!" she purred and ran on, leaving an expensive perfume lingering in the cool air.

There will always be a pair of lime-green socks in my drawer, and the great thing is that my wife knows that they are mine, and no-one else in the family would be seen dead in them.

The Peek-a-Boo Trail

David Syme

On the high south Utah plain of USA there is an 18-mile north-to-south escarpment, the lower eastern side being an amazing landscape of eroded formations of red rock – Bryce Canyon. This National Park had been on our holiday wish-list for some time and this year we made it.

You can enjoy the views from various excellent viewpoints along the rim of the escarpment, and most of the park visitors do this. Their coach deposits them for 20 minutes of snapping here, twenty minutes there, then they are whisked off to another of Utah's many beautiful parks. A smaller number of visitors descend and walk one or two of the well-made trails which weave through these dramatic rocks. Some trails are described as strenuous, others moderate or easy; all were well worth the effort. A few strings of horse-riders, too, use some of the trails, but I saw no runners.

We explored the park thoroughly. There is nothing worse than talking to someone back home who has been there, who asks where you went then tells you that you missed by far the best trail! We walked every day trail in the guidebook, saw the canyon at daybreak and at dusk, and admired the stars at night. At no time was the weather anything other than perfect.

At 3 pm on the eve of our departure my wife Pat declared that she was 'canyoned-out', and wanted to sunbathe. Fine, I said, I'll go for a run. We had walked the Peek-a-Boo trail I fancied it as a running route; now was my chance. We drove back to our motel in Tropic, a small settlement to the east of the park. From there, a few miles up a dusty road, lies a little-used trail which acts as the back door to the park. I took the rental car to the trailhead, enjoyed a long drink of water then started my run. Heavy breathing soon reminded me that I was 2,500m above sea level, so I settled into a "no heroics" gentle trot. The trail was wide and stony, but rose at a steady angle which just allowed me to keep running. After a mile and a half I branched left to start the Peek-a-Boo loop. This is also used by the horse riders; the horses know the trail well, and cleverly empty their bowels just before a steep section − a timely warning! I chose to take the clockwise route and set off up a steep slope on beautifully-constructed switchbacks. Although I had to walk some of this section I gained height very quickly and was soon looking over into Peek-a-Boo Valley. There are so many isolated red stone pillars (called hoodoos) that it would be ideal terrain for a game of peek-a-boo, I suppose. Like all other trails inside the park the smooth surface was of fine red gravel, which meant that I could confidently raise my head to admire the scenery as I ran along. The trail wound its way round outcrops of crumbling rock then plunged deep into the valley. It turned west towards the cliffs which rose sheer to the rim, and before long I hit welcome shade and cooled down somewhat. A tiny spring had been utilised to provide water for the horses, and a string was there when I passed, some of the riders using the near-by restrooms. Apart from these riders I saw very few people on my run, which added to my enjoyment of it. I was now at the far end of the loop, and from here on I started uphill again, with the rim high above on my left. Window Wall is a towering length of thin pink-grey rock; so thin, in fact, that two windows appear high up in it, each about 5 metres in diameter. The trail winds round, then through

Window Wall, Bryce Canyon

the wall at its eastern end, and it brought me to a point where the view was so fantastic that I had to stop. The main Bryce amphitheatre lay before me. Row after row of red hoodoos banked up like red giants on the terraces of a huge stadium, all afire in the early evening sunshine. I paused where a chap was sitting, in awe of the majesty of the scene. In a German accent he said: "This is just like a movie...." then words failed him! I continued round the loop. On my right I could see Wall Street, where the Navajo Trail passes through a narrow gap between two tall cliffs. Somehow two pine trees had managed to survive and grow 30 metres tall at the narrowest point, no wider than 3 metres. I was descending now, loping on a firm surface down a pleasantly angled slope, and with views to die for... this was a real runner's high! All too soon I reached the end of the loop and started down the mile and a half trail back to my car. Even although the scenery became much less dramatic I remained on that high. The slope was now ideal for a decent canter and I made short work of it. I returned to our room with a great feeling of achievement.

The plus points from this run make quite a list! Firstly, it was my only run of the week, so stood out as a high point. Secondly, the scenery was jaw-droppingly remarkable. Thirdly, I was running on such well-made trails, fourthly the weather was perfect and fifthly I had the trail to myself for the most part. We runners cover hundreds of miles as we enjoy our sport. Many of these miles are over known ground, some over new ground. Just occasionally we will run over new ground which is special. I know that it was a privilege to run the Peek-a-Boo trail, and good luck that I ran it when I did. I will remember it long after the memories of other runs have faded away.

Reborn in Borneo

Frank Tooley

Culture shock is one of the delights of travel, and the adventurous runner can make the most of it. A run in a strange environment will offer different sights and smells, climates, cultures, flora and fauna. The contrast between the south of Edinburgh and the north of Borneo was so refreshing that it seemed to invigorate and signal a new start in life. It will linger in my memory for a very long time.

Kota Kinabalu is the capital of Sabah, the Malaysian province forming the North-West tip of Borneo. Mount Kinabula at over 4000 m is the 20th tallest mountain in the world by topographic prominence. From Kota Kinabalu, the rising sun silhouettes Mount Kinabalu and that is the view that greets me as I leave the villa we are staying in for ten days whilst on a South East Asia tour. This is my regular morning run now and contrasts markedly with the runs I normally do around the Pentlands and Water of Leith which are on my doorstep in Juniper Green, the suburb of Edinburgh where I have lived for 19 years. In Scotland, dawn breaks with the sun rising over the Pentlands, the hills to the south of the City, but typically it is so cold that you run with hat and gloves, tights and two layers and often take a water proof jacket. Instead of running through puddles as normal, this morning I have the South China Sea to run beside and I only wear a pair of shorts and my racing flats.

I do the same route every morning for two weeks but it never gets boring. The villa we are living in whilst in Borneo is a few yards from a 6 km-long, white sand beach and this morning the tide of the South China Sea is nearly in so I will be running as close to the water as possible to avoid running in dry sand. I run north first with the sea on my left. The only other people out at this time of day work for the resort and are sweeping the beach clean of all that has washed up during the night.

In addition to the inevitable plastic bottles there is an interesting collection of unusual seaweed and dead sea life such as small fish and shell fish. I'm delighted to find some beautiful shells that will serve as useful souvenirs. The beach narrows as I approach its end and I decide to head back by running through the shrub. The area is populated by monitor lizards and the largest of these at 3 metres long is only slightly smaller than a Komodo Dragon. They are magnificent animals with huge claws and a darting purple tongue. I had fed one a hard-boiled egg the previous day during our breakfast buffet beside the pool. I get to the track leading back to the villa and in my path is a snake at the side of the road. I confirm that it is dead, maybe hit by a car, and not just heating itself up at the side of the road as it's just past dawn, so I give it a nudge with my trainers. One of the lizards will be along soon to hoover it up or perhaps the birds will get to the carrion first.

It occurs to me what a huge contrast this is with my runs around Edinburgh. In this climate, there are interesting insects, reptiles, birds and animals everywhere you look and the flora is similarly colourful. I'm used to never seeing anything other than midges, flies, dogs and seagulls in Edinburgh.

I proceed back to the beach to run along the surf line to the other end. The beach is home to an unbelievably large population of tiny crabs. The sand is punctured by billions of holes which vary in size from millimetre-sized to a centimetre. Beside each hole is a small sculpture of sand that the crab has created. As you run towards them they scurry sideways into their holes.

I eventually reach the South end of the beach and the sun has now fully risen. We are close to the equator so the sun rises much more quickly than I am used to at 55 degrees north in Edinburgh (on the rare occasion you see it at all). It is already starting to get too hot for running so after a quick diversion to the gym for water and a few reps on each of the weight machines and 20 minutes on the stationary bike, I run back to the villa.

To cool down, I take off my racing flats and run into the surf. I'm the only person in the sea and head out beyond the breaking waves to float looking back at the beautiful sight of the beach and palm trees in the foreground and the rainforest leading up to Mount Kinabalu in the background. This is not an option back home!

Now for a well-deserved breakfast of Bircher muesli; that's the same wherever I run!

If only I had known…

David Syme

I do not claim to know much about Albania. I went there twice, each time to conduct a one-week course to their military, but only saw the airport (small but modern and pleasant) the road to the capital Tirana (a string of shops, industrial estates and businesses dripping with advertisements, like many other airport roads) and Tirana itself. I do claim to know something of Tirana, because I ran through it every morning before work.

The tall glass and steel structure of my hotel, the Tirana International, stands in the very heart of the city. It overlooks the square with the statue of Skanderbeg, Albania's 15th-century liberator, while across the street squats the grandiose National Historical Museum. Making the scene from my window uniquely Albanian were the colourful Et'hem Mosque, the Catholic cathedral and the little old beggar who crouched on the kerb all day and played a reedy set of bagpipes. I was very happy to stay there; it was the perfect spot from which to explore the city.

On my first visit I explored in every direction. If I went to the right from the hotel I was soon on the main road to the airport which offered little of interest. Even the streets behind the main road were full of internationally known businesses – there was little of Albania to see. Going behind the hotel I soon found the railway station, but this, unusually, was not very interesting.

161

Because of its rugged terrain Albania has few rail links, and the station is a poor shadow of stations in other Eastern European capitals. This sector of the city was polluted and lacked charm, so I only explored it once. If I turned left at the hotel entrance I could follow a major road with colleges, hospitals and the military academy where our courses were held. Ahead and in the distance I would see a wooded hill with a TV mast on the top. I tried a couple of runs in the area, but kept to the streets well short of the hill. I recognised that it was too ambitious a target for a morning run, but it attracted me.

By far the most rewarding direction for morning runs was straight ahead. From Skanderbeg Square the broad, tree-lined Deshmoret e Kombit Boulevard led to Mother Theresa Square. Beyond the square lay a park with limited vehicle access. It consisted of a wooded hill with pagodas, play areas for children and exercise areas for the elderly. There was also a private school and by 0730hrs some black Mercedes cars were depositing youngsters at the gate. Beyond lay a reservoir and open country, a delightful area for my runs with plenty of variety, and so on my second visit I concentrated on it.

The start of my run always took me past Ministry buildings with sleepy police guards, then along the boulevard proper. One side opened into a grassy meadow, criss-crossed by paths. Empty in the early morning, this became a favourite haunt of young children who played with plastic toys or rode tiny electric cars later in the day. A small river passed under the boulevard in a concrete channel; I noticed that the water was clean and the channel litter-free. Further up the boulevard I passed some smart hotels, and only occasionally met other runners, who were probably non-Albanian. Two fit young men in grey sweatshirts and knee-length shorts who loped along comfortably could well have been guards from the US Embassy. On separate mornings I attacked the hill from the left, then from the right, and ran round the reservoir in both directions. As a challenge I would shun the easy boulevard route home and weave my way through side streets. Mostly, I had the park and the streets to myself. I concluded that running is not a popular sport in Albania.

My second course ended on Friday afternoon and my flight home was at 1430hrs on Saturday. I saw this empty Saturday morning as a chance to explore the inviting wooded hill to the left from the hotel. I put some money into my pocket in case a taxi ride might be needed, then set off. The first part of the route was very familiar to me, and I enjoyed that tingle of reverse culture shock: "I'm running past dusty shops and smelling exotic smells in Tirana today, but tomorrow I'll be running round Harlaw Reservoir near Edinburgh, probably in rain." Once past the military academy I was exploring new sights again. I came to a major road climbing to the shoulder of my chosen hill and slogged up it. Trucks went slowly uphill, spewing hot diesel fumes. My eyes searched out a path which went through a shanty town in the direction of the summit, so I nipped over the road and before long was running on a good uphill path through tall pines. This was more like it! Whenever a path leading higher up the hill appeared, I took it, and was looking forward to the summit when the path reached a chain-link fence. Path users before me had chosen to follow the fence line, so I did, too, hoping for a gate. Concentrating on roots, stones and holes I almost ran into the soldier who stood blocking the path. He was unarmed, and waved a cigarette downhill at me. I stopped and took in the scene. Behind the soldier a road went through the fence, and behind the road was a pill box sentry house. I nodded acceptance "Time to head for home..." I pointed to the road and he indicated that I could take it, so I jogged down it and eventually back to the hotel. Clearly a CCTV camera had tracked me and alerted the sentry to my approach – a weird feeling.

I showered, dressed and took a late breakfast, then packed and put my case into the porter's room. With a few hours to kill I sauntered along the boulevard of my favourite run. At the meadow there was a buzz of activity. Tents had been erected, loudspeakers were blaring out pop music and there were banners everywhere. Intrigued, I looked for an explanation… In one corner I saw what every runner would recognise – a line of registration tables. I picked up a leaflet in Albanian and read what I could, trying to work out what was happening. It was not too difficult; I had stumbled upon a People's Running Festival! Young runners were to do short runs up and down the boulevard, which closed to traffic shortly after I arrived, older children competed in a 5 km race, and there was a 10 km race for adults. All who had registered had start numbers and coloured ribbons and there were children rushing around in excited anticipation. Pop music gave way to an announcer who did nothing to calm the mood. He yelled instructions and during each race roared competitors on. For a moment I considered rushing back to the hotel, putting on running kit and entering, but… it had been a tough run earlier. I mingled and watched, enjoying the feeling that I was with like-minded people. The 10km field lined up at the start (my two US guards among them) and set off. There were perhaps 300 starters, with some who looked strong, but also plenty of 'have-a-go' runners at the tail. I would have enjoyed the run immensely.

I returned to my hotel with a more positive view of Albanians and running, but with the rueful thought that I had missed the opportunity of a race. I would have loved to present our club handicapper with a time from the Tirana 10km!

Post PowerPoint

David Syme

The course was held in Birmensdorf near Zurich in early October.

At the best of times PowerPoint presentations are hard to bear, and this one was 5.30–6.30 pm, at the end of a long Day 1 of the course. The joke to open the session might have gone down well on a more convivial occasion, but the titters and grins were more polite than spontaneous. The meat of the presentation was barely digestible, and the silence in response to "Any questions?" at the end spoke volumes.

Outside the classroom there was an excited buzz of conversation. Meetings in the bar were agreed, mobile phones were at every second person's ear, and there was a rustling of clothing and a clicking of briefcases. At such moments I just want to go to my room, get into my running kit and go outside, so that is what I did. I guessed that I had almost one hour of daylight and I wanted to use it all on my run. My first aim was to find an ATM for some Swiss francs, so I headed into the village centre, all the while scanning the horizon for what I craved most – a steep hill. Surely I am not alone in seeking a tough climb to brush away the cobwebs of sitting in a classroom all day? Especially after that last presentation....

I did my business at the ATM then ran through the tidy

cobbled streets until I spotted a wooded hill with a TV mast on the summit ridge. As it was fairly close to the village I kept going along the road until I was at the other side of the hill, and could return over the top. Daylight was fading, but the red warning light near the top of the mast was a welcome way-marker, and I turned confidently up a forestry track towards it. Unfortunately the trees were at least 30 metres high on both sides of the track, so I lost the comforting sight of the red light, and much of the daylight. Never mind, I thought, an extra challenge or two will help me to forget the unpleasant 'death by PowerPoint' experience.

In the twilight the simple plan I had made appeared not to be so simple. The track did not lead straight up to the ridge; it curved round the hill gently, so that I lost my orientation. Seeing a footpath which went off at an angle uphill I took it and trotted with renewed confidence. Fallen branches and brushwood in the grey light soon had me slowing down to a cautious jog, but I emerged eventually onto what I took to be the summit ridge with a track running nicely along it.

The problem now was that I was unsure whether to go right or left! Unless I climbed one of those tall trees I could not see the mast light, and my route to this point had confused my sense of direction. I went left and reached a clearing after a few minutes. There was a large board with a map of the woodland park, but by this time it was too dark for me to read. Thinking that the map might be there for walkers from Birmensdorf, I continued in the same direction. One thing made me nervous. I knew that the busy railway from Zurich to Zug ran through Birmensdorf, so I should be hearing the trains if I was heading in the right direction, but all was silent, save the hooting of an owl.

My track reached another clearing with a huge barn full of neatly piled wood, and several paths and tracks led off downhill on all sides. I had reached one end of the ridge, hopefully the

Birmensdorf end. Taking the line of the ridge I plunged down a dark narrow path and was relieved to see lights ahead. The trees gave way to houses, and in the still air I could smell some wonderful smells – a barbecue here, fried fish over there and some cinnamon and apple there! I soon identified the lights of the tennis courts, and saw the railway station ahead. I was back in Birmensdorf. The lack of train noise was also cleared up; after Birmensdorf Station the tracks entered a long tunnel! I remembered a Swiss saying: "Our country is like our cheese, full of holes".

The remainder of the run was a pleasant jog through well-lit streets, and I was able to relax. The run had done what I wanted. It had made me focus on immediate physical and mental challenges, thereby working off the tensions, the fatigue and the frustrations of a heavy PowerPoint session. I hope that those at the receiving end of the presentation cleared their heads as successfully as I, who had given it, did.

The Runs That Never Were

David Syme

Sometimes events are remarkable just because they didn't happen. This is the story of runs in Costa Rica which promised to take place but never did. All the kit was there for enjoyable runs in the tropical heat. I had packed floppy hat, sun screen, my vest top, skimpiest shorts and my lightest shoes, plus a headband and two wristbands, and I always run on holidays.

I could have run on the first morning in the capital, San Jose, but the fatigue of the two flights broken by the stress of transit through Miami International Airport provided an easy excuse. The free time later that day was another opportunity, but the strong sun beating down on concrete, the traffic pollution and lack of greenery near our hotel were too much. I did 3k on a treadmill before chilling out with a beer. That doesn't count.

Day two was mainly spent travelling, so I was looking forward to a leg-stretch when we reached our destination, the Carribean coastal national park of Tortuguero. It did not take long for me to find out that the only way into and out of our lodge was by boat. There was a 2k trail, so I explored it and found it unsuitable for careful walking, never mind jogging. That meant no running on Days 3 and 4 either. With an early start on Day 5 we left the rainforest and headed back to the interior. After a bone-jarring drive we stopped for two nights at Sarapiqui. Surely a chance for a run here? I should explain that the theme for this tour of Costa Rica was its natural wildlife. Our excellent guide noted that we were all keen on bird-watching and kindly offered 0600hrs daybreak walks, when we could all spot birds in our hotel grounds. For a runner needing his fix – a tough call, but it had to be the birds.

On the evening of Day 7 we arrived at our hotel a good hour before 6 pm darkness, and I sensed a window of time for a run. Just before slipping into the gear I turned on the TV, looking for a channel in English for my wife, Pat. What did I find but a thriller of a tennis match from the Australian Open, with our own Andy Murray on court! Change of plan – I stayed glued to the box. The next morning I enjoyed the bird-watching, confident that I would have a great chance of a run over the next two days, when we would be in the cooler cloudforest resort of Monteverde. However, the site of our hotel, El Establo, was not conducive to running. Reception and dining facilities were at the lower end of a very steep, narrow hill. Nine blocks of bedrooms were spaced out in line above, and we were in Block 8. Sure, the views were superb, but I've never yet had to take a shuttle bus to start and end a run, couldn't face the hill, and so another couple of days passed. On Day 10 we drove back to the San Jose hotel. Some were leaving the tour at this point so we had a farewell drink in the bar for them, so no evening run.

Those of us staying had opted for a five day add-on in a beach hotel at Manuel Antonio park on the Pacific. I am wary of running on beaches, as I damaged an ankle once from running along a sloping one. But... at least I would have a chance for a run with no early departures and no organised bird-watching! We drove to the coast in keen anticipation. The tour had been great, but intense. The next five days were to be the icing on the cake, each of us doing our own thing, and my thing was running.

Manuel Antonio is one of Costa Rica's most famous national parks, and it has attracted much tourist development. We were all relieved to arrive at our hotel in one piece, as our driver had taken the last few narrow, twisty kilometres at top speed. El Parador lies astride a wooded peninsula, separated from the nearest beach by tall cliffs. The only access to the beaches was on the narrow road by taxi or the hotel shuttle bus. The road was lined with hotels, restaurants, tourist offices and supermarkets; it had no pavement and was busy. The thought of running along that road frightened the life out of me! Once again I restricted my running to a couple of ks on a treadmill.

Back in San Jose we were to meet at 11 am for transport to the airport for the long journey home. Surely I could manage a quick 5–6k before breakfast and packing? It was not to be. A minor but significant attack of Montezuma's Revenge kept me close to our room until it was time to go. So, to spend 16 days on holiday without a single run could be seen as a complete blank, a disaster. My runner's conscience sums it up with: "Should have tried harder" I can't argue with that. Thankfully I was not in strict training for a race, so it did not matter. Perhaps the break from running might have been for the good, long-term.

My friend Donald was in West Africa at the same time. When we met up afterwards he told me that he hadn't run once there, either. On Day 1 in Lomé, Togo he had played an impromptu game of soccer and afterwards gifted his trainers to a young local lad, the only one who was playing barefoot.

Now, that's a better excuse for not running on holiday!

Tong-Len:

The Edinburgh Link

Tong-Len UK is a registered charity devoted to the welfare and education of destitute children in Dharamsala, Northern India. It is run by British people from a private house in Edinburgh and contributes financial and volunteer support to Tong-Len India.

From 1849 until India achieved independence in 1947, Dharamsala was a garrison town for British regiments. Its mountain air made it a popular place for officials to visit in summer, when the heat on the plains became intense. Since his flight from Tibet in 1959 it is the home in exile of the leader of Tibetan Buddhism, His Holiness the 14th Dalai Lama, and, as a leading centre for Tibetan art, craft and culture, is also a busy tourist attraction.

Rachel Owen of Edinburgh went to Dharamsala with an organisation called Volunteer Tibet in a break from her studies. She worked within the Tibetan community there, but was struck by the plight of Indian Internally Displaced Persons (IDPs). These were large communities of people who had been forced to leave their homes in other parts of India, often by drought-induced poverty, and were camped in slum settlements on the outskirts of the town. She met a Tibetan monk, Jamyang, who did what he could, asking tourists to contribute unwanted clothing and money which he used to provide flip-flops and food for the children he saw begging in the streets and scavenging in the rubbish. Jamyang had a vision to start some of these destitute children into school. Rachel wanted to help and sought support from her family. When Rachel's mother, Anna, visited in 2004, the first ten children were given their first ever opportunity of education. Initially they attended school as day pupils but after only two months the spread of disease from the slum camp to the school was such that the head teacher insisted upon residential accommodation for them if they were to continue in school. At this point it became obvious that the work required charitable status so Tong-Len was registered as a charity both in India and UK. The expression Tong-len in Tibetan language means 'giving out and taking in' and is the core of an altruistic desire to take in or share in suffering and give out happiness. Rachel and another young volunteer, Michael Blakey, worked in Dharamsala with Jamyang for several years. Michael lost his life there, the victim of a mugging. Now Anna and her husband Gareth, who live in Edinburgh, are the driving force of Tong-Len UK.

Tong-Len's first initiative was to send promising IDP children to a local English-medium school. This scheme has become very successful with several Tong-Len children achieving top marks in national exams. The sponsorship programme developed to include the most needy as well as the most able and there are now 70 children (and rising) living in safety in the two recently-constructed Tong-Len hostels which were inaugurated by His Holiness the Dalai Lama on November 19th 2011. The architect of the new hostel is the Owens' elder daughter, Dr Ceridwen Owen, who also gave all her time and expertise freely. A further 30 children can be accommodated as funding becomes available. For those children remaining in the slum camp, four Tong-Len teachers, assisted by volunteers, work in two large tents to provide a basic primary education to all school-age children. There is also a nursery/hygiene/nutrition programme for the younger children

– for most this is the first step on the long road out of poverty.

Since January 2006 Tong-Len has run a range of health clinics and disease prevention programmes in a number of slum camps in the Kangra valley. This work was started by Rachel, a graduate nurse. Tong-len also has an extensive vaccination programme, run in conjunction with government doctors.

Tong-Len is a small charity which relies on donations from friends world-wide. Volunteers of all ages and backgrounds come to work with Jamyang and his team, go home and spread the word about this initiative. The sad fact is that for every child who is supported by the charity there are many who are not.

For more information go to **www.tong-len.org**